Justice and the Judiciary

Nijhoff Law Specials

VOLUME 80

The titles published in this series are listed at brill.nl/nlsp

Justice and the Judiciary

By

Georghios M. Pikis

MARTINUS
NIJHOFF
PUBLISHERS

LEIDEN • BOSTON
2012

Library of Congress Cataloging-in-Publication Data

Pikis, Georgios.
Justice and the judiciary / by Georghios M. Pikis.
p. cm. -- (Nijhoff law specials ; vol. 80)
Includes index.
ISBN 978-90-04-23238-9 (pbk. : alk. paper) -- ISBN 978-90-04-23239-6 (e-book) 1. Justice, Administration of. 2. Procedure (Law) 3. Justice. I. Title.
K2100.P55 2012
347--dc23

2012021138

This publication has been typeset in the multilingual "Brill" typeface. With over 5,100 characters covering Latin, IPA, Greek, and Cyrillic, this typeface is especially suitable for use in the humanities. For more information, please see www.brill.nl/brill-typeface.

ISSN 0924-4549
ISBN 978 90 04 23238 9 (paperback)
ISBN 978 90 04 23239 6 (e-book)

This book is printed on acid-free paper.

I dedicate this book to justice

CONTENTS

PART I

JUSTICE

PART II

THE JUDICIARY

ACKNOWLEDGMENTS

I acknowledge the help given me by Katerina Charitou, a most charismatic person and lawyer in the transcription of the book, many intelligent suggestions and, generally, her support in going through the writing process. Also, I express my gratitude to Ioanna Constantinou, a gifted person and lawyer for the help given me in the transcription of the book and valuable comments.

To both of them I owe a debt that I am happy to acknowledge.

I do however take total and absolute responsibility for whatever is written in this book emanating from my dictations.

PREFACE

Over the years, justice has attracted many definitions. A common element of all characterisations of it, has been the measure of things, the denominator of what is good, proper and warranted by the knowledge and true understanding of the *cosmos*. Injustice denoted the opposite, what is bad, impermissible and what should be avoided. The meaning and definition of justice have been in the epicentre of philosophical thinking in relation to every sphere of life.

Justice has been viewed as a shield against derailment from the true path of life. Throughout civilisation, those in power claimed justice to be their guide even when they defied fundamental norms of it. Division of populations into slaves and free men was accepted without demure with the former classified as objects and the latter as subjects of the law. It was accepted that one man could dominate over another inevitably limiting the creative forces of humanity and undermining human dignity.

Traditional views founded on custom and often theistic beliefs gave credence to what was conceived to be superior commands.

Democracy, as conceived and practiced in Ancient Greece, was founded on the premise of total equality of citizens in all walks of life while keeping out of this category slaves and aliens inhabiting the city as well as women from participating in state affairs. This unacceptable division of the population apart, democracy premised on fundamental norms of justice – isonomy, isopolity and isocracy– functioned well. Under imperial rule that succeeded the city state in many parts of the world, democracy to the extent it found application, was confined to the centre of power as opposed to the overlorded lands. Feudalism that came to shape economic life cultivated serfdom, tying workers to the land of their masters.

Renaissance and the Enlightenment that followed gave a new perspective to just rule and discernment of the needs of humanity. The pursuit of justice and identification of its principles gained a new momentum. Reaction to the new trend was immense. I need only recount that in the mid 17th century the King of England dismissed Sir Edward Coke the Chief Justice of England for disputing his claim to rule by divine right and not by right deriving from the common law of the country. Another sad example is slavery practiced in America by white men enslaving Africans coming to the new land as a means and tool for exploring their country and cultivating their lands. With the liberation of America, division of the population into whites and blacks did not cease notwithstanding the salutary proclamations of the American Constitution as to the freedom and dignity of man. In due course, slavery was succeeded by legalising separation of blacks and whites, in the entire domain of life, based on the deceptive principle of "separate but equal". It was not until 1954 that the division ended following the decision of the Supreme Court of the United States in *Brown v. Board of Education* 347 U.S. 483 (1954), overruling a previous judgment of the same Court, notably, *Plessy v. Ferguson* 163 U.S. 537 (1896), condemning thereby the separation as violative of the principles of the Constitution.

In other parts of the world too, unjust divisions of society into separate estates persisted until modern days. The separation of Indian society into castes was another insult to humanity while the treatment of the *Untouchables* was an unqualified disgrace. Worse still was apartheid rule enforced in South Africa, defying justice to the core.

Colonisation of many parts of the world by Europeans was another source of inequality of human beings whereas the end of it was marked by bloody wars of liberation. Parallel to colonisation, spheres of influence began to be mapped by powerful nations, the Monroe Doctrine of 1823 being an apt example. The United States had declared that any intervention by external powers in the Americas—meaning in the entire continent of America—would be treated as a potentially hostile act against the U.S.A..

In countries where democracy gained ground, women were, as a rule, treated, as persons of subordinate status, essentially denied, until recent times, the right to vote. Elsewhere, women fared worse. They were regarded as possessions of the male sex.

The remedy of gross injustice in countries that adopted democracy and the rule of law at home had no corresponding impact on international relations. Big countries in terms of power, military and financial, dominated weaker ones in many parts of the world. Conflicts between states resulted in destructive wars bringing about misery to humanity on a gigantic scale. The two world wars of the 20th century left behind unprecedented human catastrophe and ruins.

The Universal Declaration of Human Rights (see Annex), adopted by the General Assembly of the United Nations on 10th December 1948, charting the way for the treaties and conventions that followed, provided a new impetus for the pursuit of justice in many areas of life. The Council of Europe and its offspring, the European Convention on Human Rights and Fundamental Freedoms and the European Court of Human Rights, and other regional institutions associated with human rights such as the Inter-American Court of Human Rights and the African Charter on Human and Peoples' Rights, gave a degree of solace to humanity at home but less so on the international scene. The world was divided into spheres of influence, acknowledging to superpowers the right to dominate weaker partners. The breakup of this development with the collapse of the Soviet Union, was an agent of relief for subordinated countries while the establishment of the European Union and its forerunners provided strong indications that the merging of different societies under common rule is not only possible but highly beneficial too.

The need for safeguarding just rule was strongly felt after the inequities of warfare that led to the establishment of world organisations to secure peace and ad hoc international courts to confront criminals who assailed humanity. The establishment of the short-lived League of Nations after the First World War and the United Nations after the Second World War were and, the latter, is still, intended to be, the guardian of peace. The Nuremburg and Tokyo tribunals established by the victors of the Secord World War after the defeat of the Axis powers to try war criminals instantiated ad hoc courts with regional jurisdiction. The advent of ad hoc courts was repeated in the years that followed with a view to bringing to justice offenders of crimes against humanity, in the wider sense, following local wars and their sequel (International Criminal Tribunal for the Former Yugoslavia, International Criminal Tribunal for Rwanda (note: the ICTY and ICTR will be replaced as from 2012–2013 by the International Residual Mechanism for Criminal Tribunals International Residual Mechanism for Criminal Tribunals), The Special Court for Sierra Leone, Extraordinary Chambers in the Courts of Cambodia, Special Tribunal for Lebanon).

The Permanent Court of Justice set up after the First World War primarily to litigate between disputing nations, collapsed, as the League of Nations did, during the prelude to the Second World War. The International Court of Justice, set up after the Second World War, trusted with a similar mandate, be it marginally extended, has had a longer life than its predecessor intended as a lasting institution whose jurisdiction will hopefully be expanded. The International Criminal Court is another international judicial body, set up by the Rome Statute concluded in 1998, endowed with jurisdiction to try persons committing acts of genocide, crimes against humanity, war crimes and the crime of aggression on a world scale.

National legal systems broadened their jurisdictions to check injustice, under the influence of human rights and adapted their judicial procedures to ensure their protection. Notwithstanding improvements noted above, warfare has not eclipsed nor have massive violations of human rights. Warfare has raged in many parts of the world leaving behind thousands of victims. The bonds of humanity are easily broken, as history tells, in pursuit of ephemeral, perceived interest.

Enhanced knowledge about cosmic order and needs for the sustenance of life and realisation of the potential of man have improved amenity to identify and define the norms of justice. At the same time it has enriched destructive armoury, making violation of the principles of justice more damaging to humanity and the environment compared to the past. What is encouraging is that an increasing number of countries proclaimed commitment to the rule of law nationally and internationally. The hope is that this commitment is not skin deep but deep rooted in recognition of the needs of humanity.

The object of writing this book is to convey my understanding of justice and its dictates and the role of the judiciary, the agent of justice, in upholding it.

PART I

JUSTICE

CHAPTER ONE

INTRODUCTION

1. From early on in my life, justice, as a concept and its expression in life and world affairs has attracted my attention as well as the foundations of just conduct. This led me to pursue the legal profession. Having studied law at London University, I sequentially became a Barrister-At-Law (Gray's Inn). I started practicing as an advocate of the Cyprus Bar at the age of 22. My dream was to become a judge and I did become a judge after 5 years of practice, at the age of 27. Thereafter, I served as a judge for about fourty three years, in Cyprus and abroad. The object of writing this book is to convey my understanding of justice and the role of the judiciary in upholding it. My knowledge derives from my legal and other studies, from my experience as an advocate of the Cyprus Bar for five years and as a judge in Cyprus and abroad for fourty three years. I served as a judge at all levels of the Cyprus judiciary, District Judge for six years, President of the District Court for nine years, Justice of the Supreme Court for over thirteen years and President of the Supreme Court of Cyprus for nine years. In 2003, I was one of the first judges to be elected to serve on the International Criminal Court, at The Hague, with a six year mandate. I was assigned to serve on the Appeals Division becoming the first president of the Chamber. I served on a full-time basis for a little more than five years. My studies were not confined to law but extended to philosophy, history, logic and dialectics in order to grasp the essence of justice.

2. During my service as President of the Supreme Court of Cyprus, I was elected and served for a few years, in parallel to my duties as a President of the Supreme Court of Cyprus, as a member of the United Nations Committee against Torture, Inhuman and Degrading Treatment at Geneva. Also, during my judicial service in Cyprus, I took part in many meetings of judicial associations and was, for a time, President of the Circle of Presidents of the European Constitutional Courts. I also served as a member of the Executive Committee of the International Association of Supreme Administrative Jurisdictions and took an active part at meetings of the Commonwealth Magistrates' and Judges' Association. Also, I participated at meetings of the Supreme Courts of the world. Moreover I served, on occasion, as an ad hoc judge of the European Court of Human Rights.

3. Identifying what is just and what is unjust in any given situation and discerning the principles of justice governing any set matter or situation has always been in the forefront of every judicial decision I took. I regard it as my duty to write what has inspired me and led me to act for so many years as a judge.

4. In the first part of the book, I shall address the concept, notion and parameters of justice from a variety of viewpoints and explore the relationship between justice and the law. Moreover, I shall consider the means and mechanisms of institutionally sustaining justice as the norm to which law should conform. Justice in this context is identified as the supreme or overriding law.

5. In the process I shall advert to causes that, over the decades and centuries, have been adverse to justice and continue to be. Justice is a wider concept, not confined to human beings. The notion of justice extends to the environment of which we and non-political animals, to use the Aristotelian phraseology, are a part. It is a complex notion than enfolds life and nature, every aspect of them.

6. The search for the exploration and identification of lasting principles of justice found expression in international and regional declarations defining the inalienable rights of man on the personal and social plane. In the 20th century, declarations, treaties, conventions and agreements giving expression to human rights were introduced, as well as Codes guaranteeing the rights of vulnerable members of society that law failed to protect adequately in the past, such as children, women and disabled persons, to mention but few.

7. The Judiciary, as the title indicates, is the institution that has evolved to minister justice. The means that society has chosen to achieve social cohesion and order in society can be identified as the nucleus of social organisation. As history informs, law often fails to meet the measure of justice and, not infrequently, defies basic principle of it. The remedy of injustice in the application of the law will be examined as well as the impact of the process of doing justice.

8. The requisites of due and proper administration of justice constitute a basic aspect of human rights. The qualifications of judges, educational and personal, have been of old, and continue to be, a vital consideration for the exercise of judicial power, identified as a mission. Constitutional law aims to ensure and safeguard perennially principles and values which

should govern life. The judiciary is the body trusted to uphold constitutional order in two respects; ensure conformity of the law to the principles of the basic law and administer the law within this framework.

9. The exercise of what are perceived as the corrective powers of the court, including the punishment of offenders, is a sensitive area that should be constantly under review, more so, as new knowledge is gained, respecting the effects of punishment over the years.

10. In view of the expansion of governmental functions on the one hand, and improved methods of secreting what is being done, on the other, it is vital to ensure that executive and administrative powers operate within the bounds of the law. This is an aspect of judicial power that constantly gains prominence and so it should, in order to sustain the supremacy of the law. The number of judges at any one time must be such as to ensure that justice is rendered expeditiously. Access to the court for claiming or defending one's rights, should be wide, as wide as their protection warrants.

11. The cost of litigation should never be allowed to become prohibitive, while legal aid should at all times be a supplement to the administration of justice.

12. Judicial institutions should be established on the world scene to enforce rules of international law, the counterpart of rules of municipal law. So far, only two permanent international judicial institutions have been established: the International Court of Justice and the International Criminal Court. Also, an international tribunal has been set up respecting the law of the sea.

CHAPTER TWO

JUSTICE

13. Justice has the same meaning in all languages. It means and denotes the doing of the right thing and refraining from doing the wrong thing. The principles of justice define what is right, that is, what is required by the norms of justice and what should be avoided or banished. History informs that the perception of justice has differed from era to era and, often, from country to country.

14. The inherent nature of human action has played little part of old in its classification as just or unjust, acceptable or unacceptable. An example is provided by the rules bearing on the use of force by one individual against another. The justice of the action was not appraised in times past by reference to the physical implications on man, but by who the assaulter and the victim were; master and slave, husband and wife, teacher and pupil, father and child.

15. Plato, as well as Theognis identified justice as the ideal that encompasses and enfolds all virtue and on that account, should map the way of life. The precept of justice in the Platonic Forms represents the immanent, unalterable and diachronic model for human action.

16. Aristotle defined justice as the pananthropic principle that should guide humans in their acts and deeds in all spheres of life. He sensed wisely, if I may say, that human passion is what derails man from the path of justice. Selfishness and egocentricity make man look at himself/herself as the entity around whom human action revolves. It activates passion to serve one's self. Passion, when shared by a powerful section of the public, is apt to deface the pursuit of justice on a grand scale whereupon equity (synonym of *epiky*), as perceived by Aristotle "reason stripped of human passion", can provide, if institutionalized, a residual, a corrective means of cleansing social order of inequity.

17. The Stoics were the first to proclaim that law should conform to the needs and accord with the hypostasis of human nature; it must therefore be anthropocentric, a concept that, in Roman times, gained prominence as the natural law.

18. Organised religion has played a dominant part, not always beneficial for man, in laying down what is proper and, sequentially just, in the form of customary or statutory law. Many religions are apocalyptic, revelatory of *logos*, the word of God. Revelation of deity is usually accompanied by the commendation of acceptance of what is revealed without questioning, including the suppression of any inquiry into the validity in terms of reason of what is passed on.

19. The middle ages, are also known as a dark era of humanity, because it stemmed the search for knowledge and the unimpeded pursuit of truth, witnessed organised church emerging as a parallel legal authority proclaiming church ethics and rule as the sole guide to what is just and proper for mankind.

20. The Enlightenment brought to the fore the benefits of free thinking and the dogmatically unobstructed search for truth in matters affecting society and the emergence and development of life on our planet. The rights of man, their identification and protection were a dominant feature of this period of light as well as the institutional means of protecting the rights of the individual.

21. In England, the rights, liberties and duties of man were the subject of the common law, the customary law of the country. This branch of the law was identified by the judiciary and given effect to alongside statutory law. Over the years, it was realised that the application of customary law and means of its enforcement did not always or inevitably yield just results. Remedial measures were necessary. These could be provided by the Sovereign, regarded as the repository of justice on earth, so citizens could apply to the King/Queen to relieve them from the imperfections and inadequacies of the law. As petitions for relief multiplied, the King appointed agents to dispense this species of justice termed "equity" from the latin "equitas" a word which incorporated in latin, the Aristotelian notion for justice "εικότης ". In the process, the exercise of equitable jurisdiction was systematized and a separate branch of the judiciary was established to administer it –the Chancery Division. By the Judicature Acts of 1870s, the common law, statutory law and equitable jurisdictions were merged, becoming part of the compass of the law with jurisdiction being vested in the courts of the country to administer both. And, where common law and equitable principles were in conflict, the latter would prevail.

22. In the continent of Europe, where, from the beginning, Roman law was widely spread, evolving into the Romano-Germanic systems of justice, the tradition gained prominence of formulating or framing statutory law in wide terms, allowing wide latitude to the judiciary in its application in the diverse and changing circumstances of life. The Justinian Institutes can be singled out as a codification of the basic principles of Roman law, providing a guide to its future development.

23. The rights of man, their identification and proclamation, became a dominant theme in the 18th century. The declaration of the Rights of Man by Thomas Payne stands out in this respect; so does the American Declaration of Independence as well as the principles that inspired the French Revolution, *liberté-égalité–fraternité*.

24. The inspiration to identify and give expression to the rights of man spread into the 19th century. In parallel, principles of international law gained ground with the conclusion of treaties, conventions and international agreements. The Concert of Europe, the offspring of the Treaty of Vienna of 1815 arrogated to itself the task of assuring the maintenance of the status quo in Europe, by reference to its ability to enforce it. The Franco-German war of 1871 led to the collapse of this order and the breakdown of what became known as the holy alliance. The war brought to the fore the havoc modern weaponry could wreak upon humanity. In its aftermath, the world community focused on ways and means to humanise the conduct of war, mitigating thereby injury and damage especially upon non-combatants. The two world wars of the 20th century shattered the world, revealing that justice and law can be readily overran when perceived interest warrants otherwise. In both wars, extermination of sections of the population was used as a means of serving the short and perceived long term interest of the embattled.

25. In the First World War, the Turks, in a planned and ruthlessly executed scheme, eliminated the vast majority of the Armenians residing in Turkey. Other non-Turkish communities living in Turkey did not fare much better. The identity of man as the core of humanity was not only ignored but derided. When Talat, a member of the triumvirate of Young Turks who ruled Turkey at the time, was confronted by Morgenthau, the American Ambassador to the sublime port, with the misanthropic act of the Armenian genocide replied "why should you care being an American of

Jewish origin?" to which the Ambassador responded: "I am a human being".

26. The disdain of the allies, *entente cordialle,* reflected in a statement of 1915, that those responsible for the Armenian's slaughter would face the consequences when time comes, was wholly forgotten. The victorious allies concentrated on their then current interests as defined after the war, ignoring justice as the pursuit of the civilised world. In the Treaty of Lausanne of 1923, provision was made that crimes committed by the Turks in the First World War be ignored; and none was prosecuted. Amnesty was granted cultivating the belief that even genocide can be written off.

27. The League of Nations established after the First World War trusted with responsibility to ensure world peace was short-lived. National interest and war, as a means of asserting it, supplanted both justice and peace as the guide to the resolution of disputes between states. Taking the law into their hands was the chosen way of the Germans and their allies, wholly disregarding humanitarian principles and ethics. The Permanent Court of Justice founded in the aftermath of the First World War was given little chance to resolve interstate conflicts by reference to international law.

28. The Second World War, started by the Germans under Nazi leadership, was foreshadowed by the secret treaty concluded between Germany and the Soviet Union in August 1939 to invade and partition an independent state, Poland. The war waged by the Axis powers, brought human misery and destruction on an unprecedented level. A whole ethnic group, the Jewish people were specifically targeted and nearly six million of them were annihilated. The destruction of the Jewish people was characterised as a holocaust from the Greek word *ολόκαυστον – holokauston* signifying the burning of the whole. The atrocities of the Germans were not confined to the Jews; they extended to other nationalities of occupied countries causing death, hunger and destruction on a grand scale.

29. The world was awakened to the need of addressing human disaster and humiliation on an institutional basis. The establishment of the United Nations in 1945 with the extended powers conferred upon the Security Council to undertake, whenever necessary, military action in furtherance to the United Nations' objectives was a step forward. The power to impose sanctions on wrongdoing states was another tool in the same direction, aimed to coerce the ill doers to turn to the right path. Power to authorise drastic steps for the sustenance of justice and peace was entrusted to the Security Council, a fifteen-member body of the United Nations. The war

victors and, later, China, became permanent members of the Security Council. The gravest drawback of the arrangements made for the sustenance of justice and peace was the right conferred upon each one of the permanent members to veto decisions of the Council. The onset of the Cold War and division of the world in two domains, acknowledging to each camp, supremacy in its sphere of influence, was a grave setback to the mission of the United Nations. Thus, the UN was unable to stem wars and military conflicts that erupted in different parts of the world. This diminished the authority of the United Nations as an agent of justice and peace.

30. The greatest contribution of the United Nations to justice was the adoption by the General Assembly of the Universal Declaration of Human Rights of 1948. For the first time in history, a world assembly recognised the inherent rights of man to be enjoyed and exercised at all times and in all circumstances, independently of individual characteristics, ethnicity, social position, gender or colour. Endowing each individual with the same rights is the bedrock of human rights. Equality extends to every aspect of private and social life. Implicit in the concept of human rights are the duties imported therewith to respect the corresponding rights of fellow human beings. Breach of them exposes the defaulter to civil and penal sanctions. Human rights are defined by reference to the status of man as a distinct entity and the duty of corporate institutions, trusted to uphold social cohesion and take collective action to uphold them in a democratic context.

31. Human rights are premised on the norms of justice, exercised in the context of democratic rule. Democracy emerged as a political system in Ancient Greece. First in Ionia under the name of *Isonomy*, sequentially adopted in Athens and other Greek cities under the name of Democracy, premised on three pillars: Isonomy, Isocracy, Isopolity. The three concepts underlined the equality of citizens in every sphere of individual and political life. It thus appears that democracy emerged as a political system founded on basic principles of justice; the offspring of the pillars of human rights.

32. Although the Universal Declaration of the UN was not binding on member states, it paved the way forward leading to regional treaties and conventions, guaranteeing human rights of the citizens of vast areas of the world: the European Convention on Human Rights, the Interamerican Convention of Human Rights and the Rights of African people, provide evidence of that.

33. The Universal Declaration of Human Rights is not exhaustive of the basic rights of man, a fact confirmed by many subsequent international treaties and conventions, acknowledging the rights of vulnerable sections of the public such as children, including children born out of the wedlock, disabled persons, women and other members of the community in a disadvantageous position. Civil and political rights, in their expanse, are also the subject of treaties, mostly initiated by the United Nations. The International Covenant of Civil and Political Rights is an apposite example.

34. Neither the proclamation of human rights nor their guarantee in different parts of the world have so far made the individual, on a global basis, the autonomous social unit, the standard bearer of human rights. The reasons are many. In a number of countries, women are still considered as subordinate or inferior to men, children are regarded as the ownership of the family and the use of force is admissible to achieve dubious ends. Doctrines antagonistic to human rights or aspects of them find favour among many ruling classes.

On the other hand, countries vociferously committed to human rights, show little interest in their adoption elsewhere especially in countries locked in warfare, leaving the impression that interest in conjunction with dominance is their guide to world affairs, not commitment to human rights. The impression is that their commitment to human rights is skin deep.

CHAPTER THREE

JUSTICE AND THE LAW

35. Law is at the nucleus of social organisation. It lays down the rules by which persons should function in the community, individually and collectively. The Ancient Greeks portrayed Justice as the mother of Peace. The law is the agent of justice, designed to ensure that its principles find expression in every sphere of life. Sustenance of order is the common denominator of law finding application under different legal systems.

Indeed, political systems of different characteristics have been evolved over the years, gaining their name from the philosophy that inspired them. Thus we have had monarchic, oligarchic, party-dominated, plutocratic, dictatorial and democratic systems of government.

36. Democracy, especially direct, is the most anthropocentric system of government apposite to the individuality of man, equality of status in society and the emergence of common institutions through freedom of choice of the monads making up the multitude.

37. Justice is the norm to which the law should conform and embody in every area of private and public action. Over the years and centuries, various institutions and associations claim to be repositories of justice. Religious authorities in the first place, by reference to theistic commands often revealed by "holy scriptures", and in the second, social and political doctrines importing principles perceived as immanent charting the course of life.

38. There are many such doctrines ranging from anarchic, existentialist, cooperative, totalitarian and aristocratic. These doctrines derive from philosophical schools of thought claiming, as a rule, infallibility. Plato pronounced wisdom gained through knowledge as the guide to identify what is just. According to Aristotle, reason is the guide to identifying justice, reason stripped of human passion. Reason is the greatest or superior faculty of man that enables the being, after due inquiry, to evaluate what is just and prescribe it as the law governing any given situation. Implicit in the Aristotelian conception of justice is the suppression, ideally to the point of extinction, of the uncontrolled zoic desires, arousing passion for pleasure and domination of fellow human beings, conduct antinomous to reason.

39. In their breadth, principles of justice encompass an area of zoic and political action charting the plane of their application. Law confers rights and imposes obligations, it regulates their exercise and identifies the means for their protection and, in the case of responsibilities, their enforcement. Also, it makes provision for the exercise of governmental power and the rules to which it should adhere. Ideally, the aim of the law is to formalise justice as a living institution to which obedience is owed.

40. There has been no unanimity as to the principles or norms of justice and the field of their application. However with the onset of Enlightenment, the impact of the American Declaration of Independence and the founding principles of the French Revolution *liberté, égalité, fraternité,* the rights of man gained prominence as a distinct feature of justice. The shackles on man imposed by superiors in terms of power, wealth or privilege and their removal became a major objective of a large section of society.

41. The Franco-German war of 1871 brought to the fore the capacity of man, acting singly or as part of a group, for the distraction of fellow humans their humiliation and uprootment. Suppression of the expression of such tendency became another aspect of human rights in need of protection. The establishment of principles governing the conduct of war with emphasis on the protection of civilian population gained momentum.

42. Education is vital for the development of man's capabilities. Knowledge is what broadens one's horizon enabling the individual to perceive reality in its true dimensions. The opening of educational avenues and the provision of necessary facilities are important factors for the ascent of man. The right to education is safeguarded as an indispensable human right. Knowledge, in turn, encourages the search for truth in every field of life. An imperishable debt is owed to those who, in the course of history, laid the foundations of philosophy, science, principles of humanitarian law and history. What cannot be overlooked is that knowledge in misanthropic hands can also be a source of destruction, as the history of modern era especially reveals. This is an evil against which humanity, indeed the world in its entirety, must protect itself.

43. The protection of man as an individual and as a social entity is at the epicentre of human rights. Sustenance of the individual and support of his/her potential of physical and mental development is the guide to the configuration of the rights of man. Ensuring the well being of man is at the root of the identification of human rights. The Ancient Greeks deified both Justice and Peace casting the latter as the daughter of the former

intonating thereby that peace cannot be founded on injustice and iniquity.

44. Human rights are designed to uphold the physical, social and spiritual environment within which man must live. Eudemonism is inherent in the concept of human rights.

45. Securing human nature as a physical and social entity ensures a meaningful existence and paves the way for the advancement of man. Freedom of movement and thought and the guarantee of bodily integrity as well as the existence of judicial institutions to sustain his/her rights, release the creative forces in man for the benefit of the individual and society simultaneously. Acknowledging and effectively upholding human rights is just for the individual and the collectivity.

46. Life is largely dependent on the preservation of the natural environment and its improvement. For the sustenance and, where possible, improvement of life in general, human life in particular, endowed with a higher faculty of reason, protection of nature is vital for earthly existence. Human rights is the key to the creativity and prosperity of man and happy co-existence. From this perspective, human rights incorporate salient norms of justice subject to the following: The protection afforded, is primarily seen in the context of domestic law. Attention must be focused on the globalisation of human rights as human nature warrants. Human rights are meant to uphold human existence wherever it may be, independently of distinctions. It is heartening that, in regions of the world such as Europe, America and Africa, human rights are incorporated in treaties or conventions binding member states to enforce them. In parallel, judicial institutions are established for regional protection such as at the European Court of Human Rights, the InterAmerican Court of Human Rights and the African Court on Human and Peoples' Rights.

47. The world is not static. As Heracletus asserted, motion is unstoppable leading to the conclusion that everything flows, the world being in a state of flux. New challenges to the sustenance of human rights emerge in the course of time, especially technological advances that often expose the hypostasis of man and the environment that surrounds the individual to perils that should be addressed by reference to fundamental norms of justice. This is one of the reasons why human rights should be defined in the broadest terms, warranted by existing knowledge of foreseeable needs for protection. Detailing the rights of man in specific areas, such as the International Covenant for the Protection of Civil and Political Rights in

the area of human action is a welcome development. Acknowledgment of human rights is one thing, incorporation in the legal system as inalienable, is another. To sustain their inalienability, human rights must be incorporated in the Constitution or basic law of a state binding on the legislative authority in the enactment of statutory law and the executive in the administration of it. Judicial authorities must give expression to the law, statutory and customary, subject to such modifications, as necessary to accord with the rights of man. The conferment of jurisdiction upon judicial authorities to declare laws, rules and regulations unconstitutional for breach of human rights is crucial. This is the hallmark of an effective constitutional order. Access to the court for the vindication of the rights of man is a basic requisite for their protection. Recourse to the court must be within the easy reach of the individual, a part of the armoury of the law for the protection of human rights. Lack of means should never be allowed to impede access to the court. Legal aid for the impecunious is a basic right of which man cannot be stripped. Unimpeded access to the court is also warranted by the principle of equality before the law and the administration of justice.

48. Human rights import corresponding duties to respect the human rights of others. This is an incident of the universality of human rights. Breach of the rights of man entails an obligation on the part of the violator to restore them by remedial action that may take a variety of forms. A person whose human rights are violated by anyone, be it an individual, a corporate body or the state, is entitled to redress through the process of the law. Violation of bodily integrity, hypostasis and the private and family domain of man confers upon the victim a right of action for pecuniary loss and equitable (moral) damages. Moreover, violation of the rights of man to fair treatment by those in authority confers a right to the individual to seek judicial review of the antinomous administrative action with a view to stemming illegal action or abuse of executive or administrative power. It is significant to note, that since Napoleonic times, a system of judicial review of executive and administrative action emerged in France acknowledging a right to the person affected thereby to seek judicial review of executive, with some exceptions, and administrative actions and omissions.

49. The criminalisation of action and deeds aims to punish violence against a human being and conduct grossly offensive to his/her rights undermining the status of the individual as an autonomous social unit. The prosecution of crime is nowadays regarded as a responsibility of the

public represented by the appropriate, for the purpose, authority of the state. Prosecution of crime is no longer regarded as the responsibility of the victim, which was the case in days passed. At the same time, a right to a private prosecution should at all times be sustained, enabling the victim to take the matter to court in face of inaction on the part of public authority. This is an aspect of liberty that cannot be bypassed. Ultimately, human rights enshrined in a constitution as an overarching principle of justice define the parameters of the law.

50. Exceptions to human rights, if at all permissible under the basic law, can only be sanctioned by the legislature. Only dire necessity, attributable to a cause for which exception to human rights is permissible, can be upheld by a court of law. And like every exception to a rule, relevant legislative provisions must be strictly construed and last no longer than necessity warrants. Most human rights admit of neither exception nor restriction. Nor can a human right be waived by the vestee. Such a waiver constitutes alienation of self. Human rights are definitive of the realm of man as a physical and social entity.

51. Meting out justice and the principles governing its administration are among the basic norms of human rights. The right to a fair trial will be explored in the chapter dealing with the Judiciary.

52. The Administration is equally bound to assure the fair treatment of the individual in its entire field of competence. The right to equality entails like treatment of every person in the same position. Rules have been developed to ensure the exercise of administrative power in a manner compatible with the rights of man. Equality before the law binds the Administration to treat homogenous subjects and objects of the law in a similar way. Ensuring equality before the law is the unqualified duty of every authority of the state. To ensure equality in this context too, the decision makers must have the attributes of subjective and objective independence and impartiality. The Administration must carry out an inquiry designed to elicit every relevant aspect of the subject under consideration and reason its decision, disclosing thereby its foundations and the process leading to taking it. Reasoning a decision by reference to facts and to applicable principles of law, is a safeguard against capriciousness and arbitrariness and a mark of objectivity. Apart from the right to judicial review to test the validity of administrative action, independent authorities must be set up with a mandate to ensure that the Administration operates within the framework of the law, in consonance with human

rights. The Office of the Ombudsman, first established in Sweden, could be entrusted with the task, without implying that other institutions with a similar mandate cannot be established as justice may require.

53. Human rights are to my understanding, premised on the following edict: what befits man befits the collectivity. Freedom of thought, freedom of action, abstinence from intruding into the domain of the right to private life. The collectivity too, represented as a rule by its deputies in authority, should function within the compass of human rights. Its power must be exercised with due regard to the fundamental rights of man. In much the same way as the conduct of man may become the subject of judicial scrutiny, the actions of state authorities should likewise be subject to judicial review.

54. The political side of man is expressed through direct participation in the governance of the *polis*, the city. The will of the whole is defined by the individual choice of every person. The individual is not submerged in the multitude but constitutes a component part of it. This was the prototype of democracy established in Ancient Greece entitling the citizen to participate in the communal assembly, the decision-maker on every subject, including choice of the archons, usually for the period of one year. The brevity of the mandate of the rulers was consistent with the ever present element of choice of government. Rule making, legislation, was likewise subject to approval by the citizens of the *polis*. In the domain of justice large juries of five hundred and one, chosen by lot, were assigned the task of deciding civil and criminal cases. In public assemblies, *Εκκλησία του Δήμου* (*Ecclesia tou Demou*) in Ancient Athens, an equal right was acknowledged to every participant to express his views and propagate his cause. A shortfall of the system was that women were excluded from participation. The majority determined the decisions to be taken but the brevity of the Office of the Archons insured that they did not acquire a stake of their own, providing room for the perpetuation of their dominant position. The confinement of the right to participate to citizens and the sufferance of the institution of slavery were offensive to the principle of equality and antinomous to the nature of man. Humans have the same needs for survival, well-being and advancement. The autonomy of man is the best recipe for a meaningful contribution of the individual to himself/herself and the societal whole.

55. When the city immersed in a bigger whole, the state and citizenship expanded, as increased numbers of people rendered difficult the direct participation of the citizenry in the election of rulers and direct screening

of their actions; representative democracy emerged. In due course political parties sprung with a governmental agenda.

Over the years, different systems of government came into being. To begin, the parliamentary system of government where the executive is elected by representatives accountable to the assembly. Another system that gained prominence is the presidential system under which, the executive and the legislative branches of government are separated, each directly elected by the public. The election of representatives by sections of the public belonging to organised political parties, has inevitably narrowed down choice.

56. Party government is another system, giving rise to representatives elected by a party deemed to be committed to the right cause and on that account, deriving the right to rule. This is an eclectic system of government tending to distinguish between members of the public confining rule makers and government to a select section of it in direct breach of human rights. Such a system of government is often characterised as "the dictatorship of the ruling class". It alienated a large section of the public from decision-making treating the edicts of the party as sacrosanct.

Such systems are founded on doctrines, purporting to embody the ultimate truth. They can justifiably be labelled as monolithic systems of government. Institutional justice in systems of this character is not dissociated from party rule. The doctrine to which such systems of government adhere dictates the measure of justice.

57. The enlargement of the functions of central authorities in the modern era and the complexities of governmental functions obscured by advanced technological means makes it difficult for the ordinary citizen to follow the transaction of public affairs. In fact a large section of the public is alienated from the affairs of the state, a fact evidenced inter alia by the great percentage of abstention at general and local elections. It is no overstatement to say that the apathy of the public towards the affairs of the body politic steadily increases, a fact that should awaken the guardians of democracy to the perils inherent in this tendency. In view of this development, it is imperative to establish independent institutions to scrutinise the affairs of government and report to the public. Secret services developed into estates of their own. Intelligence gathering and selective interpretation of it, is another obstacle to democracy, pregnant with dangers.

58. Only a system assuring transparency of action of public authorities is compatible with the rights of man. Information about governmental

management of public affairs is essential for the effectiveness of the rights of man to determine through his/her will, be it indirectly, who should rule.

59. A related right, the right to education providing man with the necessary knowledge to appreciate and evaluate the political scene and make an informed choice, is equally essential. Knowledge and the cultivation of the critical faculties of man is what frees the person from prejudice and enables reason to guide the individuals in the conduct of their affairs. In Plato's *Republic,* the guardians of the state, those entrusted to rule and sustain the fundamentals of the *polity* should receive education in the various fields of knowledge, gymnastics, music, philosophy, science and dialectics until the age of fifty. This may underestimate the value of daily experience in the various fields of life but rightly underlines the value of knowledge for which there is no substitute in the management of public affairs.

CHAPTER FOUR

JUSTICE AND HUMAN RIGHTS

60. The word "justice" derives from the Latin term *justitia* emanating from the Latin word *justus* meaning doing the right thing. The Greek concept of justice is itemised by the word *δικαιοσύνη* the offspring of *διχέω* meaning to divide according to entitlement. A person is just if he/she does the right thing and refrains from wrongdoing. Socrates pronounced that it is best to suffer injustice rather than do injustice. In the latter case you bear responsibility for doing wrong whereas in the former, man is free of blame.

61. The notion of justice is based on the autonomy of man and awareness and respect for the rights of others. What is right then? The answer is what befits human nature as an indivisible whole. What does befit human nature? This is not the easiest of questions. Attempting to answer it we must go back to the inseparable twin nature of man: zoic and political. Looking after one's physical and mental capabilities is beneficial for man. Seeking and gaining knowledge about the sustenance of a healthy existence is a duty to one' s self and must be welcome. Association with others, in a multitude of contexts, is another significant need of humanity. What is right is what is beneficial to the individual and in no way harmful to others. The conception of what is right in this area is apt to be highly enriched by the acquisition of knowledge, imparting the truth about a state of affairs or an aspect of life. The same goes for sharing information concerning things of common interest, mostly about scientific, philosophical, ontological matters and the public state of affairs. Sharing experiences is likewise beneficial. In this way, the offspring of knowledge and experience is spread to the benefit of mankind. Commitment to truth, associated with freedom from prejudice is a basic tenet of justice, enabling humanity to appraise what is right or wrong from a reliable perspective.

62. Human rights aim to safeguard man, every man, as a distinct entity. Human rights is a complex concept. It does not merely ensure the individuality of man in its realm but also the discharge of corresponding duties to fellow human beings and the state for their unobstructed enjoyment. The rights that befit one individual are the same as those that befit

a fellow human being. Freedom of action of an individual must not collide with or intrude into the corresponding rights of any other person. One's human rights must be exercised and enjoyed in harmony with the parallel rights of a fellow human being. Consequently human rights impose, in addition to the conferment of rights, a duty to respect the parallel rights of fellow human beings breach of which exposes the defaulter, be it an individual or the state, to sanctions, civil and/or criminal, depending on the nature of the violation and the injury occasioned thereby. A duty also arises to protect the environment and, where possible, improve it in harmony with the protection of natural life from foreseeable dangers. Man is, after all, the offspring of nature that provides the feeding ground of every existence.

CHAPTER FIVE

JUSTICE AND HUMAN NATURE

63. Justice is not confined to human rights. It extends, in the first place, to our dealings with others such as exchanges and generally in the sharing of life as well as the planning of the future. Protection of the environment and the planet in general is attuned to life according to nature. Man is a planetary being, who, like other existences, deserves respect and protection. So does the environment. The right to ownership of land does not diminish the responsibility for the use of it in a way congenial to the environment. The shaping of the environment, the cleanliness of the atmosphere and the restriction of obnoxious fumes and noises in a habitat must be attended to. The saying "live and let live" reflects human propriety that should characterise everyone's action.

64. Informed self-awareness and commitment to truth temper passion that may overpower man in the pursuit of pleasure and self-aggrandisement. Reason tells what is right. Adherence to it tends to eliminate prejudice. Sympathy for others is an incident of just conduct. On the other hand, egocentricity, that is, canalising one's action exclusively according to self-interest, in other words, viewing the world as revolving around one's self, is an agent of injustice. Because it ignores and defies the rights of others. Education is highly instrumental to the improvement of the noetic powers of man. Every form of prejudice, be it racial, ethnic or religious must be contained and, if possible, eliminated for it breeds hatred and is discordant to human harmony, philanthropy.

65. The political nature of man, the proclivity of the individual to live with others, enables humans to benefit from one another by uniting forces in the pursuit of knowledge and social good. History tells that sharing knowledge and experience and building together elevates human existence to the benefit of everyone. Human autonomy is designed to shield individual existence from intruders, not estrange man from either neighbourly or public pursuits through the multiplication of forces. It is just to give expression to every facet of human nature: children are cared for by their parents, schooled by their teachers; sharing and mutual assistance enhance human potential, a key to the realisation of the human ideal.

66. Justice, as earlier stated, is not confined, so far as the individual is concerned, to actively doing what is right, but also to refrain from doing what is right, often reflected in indifference to the fate of a neighbour. Doing wrong to a fellow human being is unjust reprehensible in every sense meriting restoration through the mechanisms of justice. Respect for the rights of others and leaving room for their meaningful enjoyment is an emblem of justice. Such acts are not only beneficial to others but create the prerequisites for corresponding respect for the good doer's own rights. Every just act has the potential of benefiting others. Such expectation should not be the motive for acting justly but a reminder that a just act has invariably beneficial consequences. Acting justly is good for anyone's self and to the benefit of everybody else. This is emphasized by the right to life importing a duty on the part of everyone, including the state, not to foreseeably expose to danger the life of any fellow human being.

67. Envy and jealousy are often the agent of misery for the person harbouring it and a moving force for doing harm to others. It breeds hatred and not infrequently leads to malicious acts. The aphorism of the Delphic oracle-know thyself- is a sound counsel for not engaging in unjust action. This is the process of gaining enlightenment about one's motivation for action enabling the individual to hold back from injuring others, by word or deed. Power trusted to a person is invariably a subject to be inquired into, especially in relation to the manner it is exercised. The epigram "power corrupts, absolute power corrupts absolutely" is not without substance though not wholly correct. Béas of Priene one of the seven sages of Greek antiquity proclaimed «αρχή άνδρα δείξει» (the exercise of power will reveal the true nature of the individual –*archi andra deixei*). The exercise of power by those in authority is a crucial domain with direct implications on justice.

CHAPTER SIX

JUSTICE AND CONSTITUTIONALISM

68. Excess or abuse of power transcends authority prescribed by law and leads inevitably to injustice. Excess of power is manifested when the vestee of authority, the holder of a position with power to decide, exceeds the limits of his/her mandate. Abuse occurs when the authority trusted to the holder of a position in the state is used for purposes other than those for which it is bestowed. In either case authority is used outside the realm of the law within which the official must function. This is wrong. Law abiding is an edict of justice for the fruition of the common ends of humanity.

69. By violating, ignoring or bypassing the law, the official assumes power he/she does not possess, making the individual or groups of persons the masters instead of the servants of the law, conduct outside the path of justice.

70. A law deviating from or falling short of what justice warrants must be retracted or amended in a manner conforming to the legally ordained process and the ends of justice. Unavailability of means to contest the law as contradictory to or falling short of the commands of justice provides compelling ground for changing the rules governing access to the court. There is much to be said for the Roman *actio popularis* legitimising every citizen to contest a law on grounds of injustice.

71. Law is the nucleus of social organisation. It sets down the rules by which human beings should live side by side in society sharing common things and participating in communal affairs. The law establishes the parameters of societal order, identifies the authorities entrusted with the governance of the state and specifies the rights and duties of members of society.

72. Over the years, several types of political regimes have emerged: a) *monarchy*, signifying rule by the sovereign and his, and rarely her, descendants, b) *oligarchy* denoting rule by select few, c) *monolithic party rule*, d) *aristocracy* which, in its original Greek meaning meant rule by those who distinguished themselves by excellence in spirit and/or deeds, e) *plutocracy*, rule by the wealthy, implying that riches are a source

of power, f) *dictatorship*, rule by command of the person or persons in power and, lastly, g) *democracy*, another Greek word, signifying rule by the people, to be precise, in its original sense, rule by the citizens of the *polis*. Anarchy must also be mentioned, signifying living without rule.

73. One may treat democratic rule as best suited to human nature. It treats the individual as the pivotal unit of society. It denotes equality in every sphere of life, in the public and private domain, on the one hand, and accountability of those exercising authority to the public on the other. Democracy was first founded as a political system befitting human nature in Ancient Greek Ionia, under the name *Isonomy*, that is, equality before the law. It emerged as the offspring of justice. It was renamed in Athens, as democracy founded on three pillars of justice, namely *isonomy, isopolity and isocracy*. It can be argued that the emergence of democracy in ancient Greece was the offspring of justice, save that it was not universal (leaving out women and slaves). It was modelled on the principle of direct participation, not only in the choice of the rulers but also in the fashioning of the law and in deliberations for the vital affairs of the polity such as going to war. Democracy was reborn in the modern era, as the form of government ensuring rule by the people. It evolved into a system of representative democracy, that is, rule by those chosen by the public. In modern times, political parties came into being with a governmental agenda, formulating propositions for decision making while acknowledging the right to any group of persons to form new parties. The aspiration or the *raison d'être* of every law is that it is just, recognising that a law falling short of justice is injurious to humanity. In fact, it came to be recognised that principles of justice should be incorporated into a basic law, a constitution, establishing the framework of rule in society. Also, judicial institutions were established to oversee the enforcement of the law, with a view to ensuring that there is no excess or abuse of power in its application.

74. Equality before the law and the administration of justice is a basic norm of democratic rule. The judiciary is trusted as the guardian of justice. It must be vested with power to remedy injustice and repudiate laws offensive to justice within the framework of its constitutional powers.

75. Law regulates the daily affairs of man. One can say that it is a reasoned guide to human action. Inconsistency of a legal norm with what justice warrants in any given situation often gives rise to insoluble conflicts unless mechanism is provided for testing its compatibility with principles of justice.

76. The role of the judiciary in the application of the law is crucial to the immersement of the law into justice. It is essential that the basic law should provide that, in identifying the parameters of a law, in interpreting and applying it, the judiciary should be guided by the fundamental principles of justice. Where doubts are expressed about the conformity of the law to the ends of justice, procedure should be put in place for seeking the opinion of supreme judicial authority on the subject. In fact, there should be mechanism, whenever necessary, for preventive justice, that is, procedural means must be provided for reference of the constitutionality of a law to supreme judicial authority before its promulgation. There is a variety of ways that could be adopted to address this need. One way of achieving this is to invest an independent office of the state with power to contest the constitutionality of a law *a priori* whenever there is uncertainty about its conformity to the basic law or the constitution. Any form of favour in the application of the law is by definition antithetical to justice. Such conduct must be proscribed in the severest terms. Officers of justice abusing their position are unpardonable.

77. Procedural rules must be attuned to the principles of a fair trial, ensuring a) speediness in the transaction of judicial causes, b) elicitation of the position of either party to the dispute in civil and administrative proceedings and c) acquainting the accused of the case he/she will have to confront at the trial. The presumption of innocence moulds the parametres of criminal procedure.

78. Justice embodies the norms that should govern life in all its manifestations. Law is par excellence the authority that defines and regulates the conduct of man in society. In the absence of rules governing societal order, chaos would prevail to the detriment of everyone. Law and its application are the instruments of justice. Justice cannot be achieved without the law. An unjust law defeats its purpose. It is no coincidence that the authority trusted as the guardian of the law, the judiciary, takes its name from justice, a reminder to all that its mission is to do justice.

CHAPTER SEVEN

JUSTICE AND MORALITY

79. In daily parlance justice and morality are used interchangeably denoting right conduct or a righteous person. Social *ethos*, ethics, should be modelled along the dictates of justice or, better still, they should reflect the norms of justice. Historically justice and morality have not always coincided. Religious ethic, superstition and doctrines proclaiming transcendental values often commit people to ethics antagonistic to equity and antinomous to reason. Attribution to natural forces of extraordinary qualities and fear of consequences of the unknown often feed superstition. Religions, filling the gap of the unknown with hyper-human forces have often led to moral rules at odds with justice. In addition, they have curtailed research about natural forces and their impetus, depriving man of essential knowledge about the cosmos. Religious establishments evolved moral rules best suiting their authority. At times, questioning their ethics was classified not only as a sin but as a crime too, punishable with severe sentences including ostracism and death. The night of Saint Bartholomew (572c.e.) is a living example of the savagery to which religious fanaticism can lead. The "Holy Inquisition" is another example of the debasement of humanity in the hands of ill-guided ecclesiastical authorities. And all this despite the basic message of Christianity, of love for fellow human beings independently of origin or denomination, sharing things between one another and even, love for enemies, barring the use of force under any circumstances. Desdemonia is not only an incident of the Middle Ages. One need only remind of Socrates, the wise, in Ancient Greece, who was sentenced to death, required to drink the hemlock accused of introducing new daemons corrupting thereby the youth, leaving a stigma on Athenian civilisation.

80. Political doctrine propounding infallibility in its pursuits and, consequently, commitment to monocratic rule has also established rules of morality offensive to justice. Adoption of such a doctrine as the state rule leads to authoritarianism, a symptom of claimed infallibility, eventually producing distortion of reason and injustice on a grand scale in the governance of the state. Like religious authoritarianism, it leads to disruption of the pursuit of knowledge and suppression of freedom of thought

and expression. Man is constrained in the pursuit of truth and alienated from his/her inborn nature in this respect. Fear of consequences often nourishes the conventional force of morality. Of all the regimes, democracy based on human values is closer to justice because it caters for the freedom of man and underlines common effort in the pursuit of knowledge and what is right.

81. Sexual conduct is a much-debated subject of morality. In the fashioning of rules of sexual behaviour, religion played a dominant part; female virginity before marriage being regarded as sacrosanct but not male virginity before marital ties. On the contrary, premarital virginity of men was regarded as a negative encouraging female prostitution on a grand scale. Monogamy was the norm prescribed by many religions. In others, polygamy was permitted, as the privilege of man. In either case, female adultery was treated as a mortal sin punishable in some societies with death. The male, in whom power resided in society, was the master to whom wife and children owed blind obedience. Admonishing and beating up wife and children by the husband and father was not only accepted in some societies but religiously tolerated too. The phenomenon is still present in some societies.

82. The Renaissance gave birth to a new era witnessing the resurgence of the pursuit of knowledge, first and foremost, by uncovering the Ancient Greek philosophical, scientific and ontological world, destroyed or hidden during the Christian era of the Middle Ages. The blackout was generated by the ecclesiastical edict "believe without searching" and the postulate that cosmic truth has been revealed.

83. The Renaissance renewed the pursuit of truth, liberating man from previous sentimental and religious constraints, sufficiently to enable humanity to move up to the sequential era of Enlightenment, advocating commitment to truth in the search for knowledge as the guide to life creating the conditions for the ascent of man in all spheres of life. The urge for equality of the two sexes in all walks of life contributed to the acknowledgment of human rights as a principal goal of human societies. It may be reminded that even in advanced societies, the right to vote was denied to women until recently.

CHAPTER EIGHT

JUSTICE AND PEACE

84. The Ancient Greeks deified both Justice ("Themis") and Peace ("Eirini") casting the former as the mother of the latter. Peace is envisioned as the offspring of justice in every facet of life, domestically and internationally. Peace, in this context, signifies harmonious coexistence free from the perils of injustice that downgrade human nature. Peace must not be confused with order as such in any one domain, that is to say, the absence of manifested conflict. Order may be imposed, and often is imposed, by coercive means that invariably explode in the pursuit of justice. I think that history confirms that plasmatic order does not qualify as a state of affairs amounting to peace. On the contrary, it breeds contempt and arouses enmity towards the regime both on the national and international plane. The Nazi regime under Hitler and the Soviet regime under Stalin provide apt examples of plasmatic peace.

85. Peace is meaningful only when the rights of man, as an autonomous social entity, are respected including the right to participate and have a voice in societal and governmental affairs. Peace of mind has as a prerequisite the availability of support for those in need and assurance of the safety of the individual, freedom of thought, expression and movement. Equality of individuals before the law and equality of treatment by every state authority or institution are basic attributes of peace. Peace is meaningful when infused with the fundamentals of justice releasing the creative forces of man in every direction. My reading of world history suggests that human progress is directly dependent on the extent to which order is fashioned by what befits humanity in every aspect of life.

86. Once the mantle of justice is cast over man the individual is capable of infinite achievement, in every sphere of life. Peace founded on justice, paves the walk of life diachronically.

87. It is no coincidence that within a relatively short time, in Ancient Greece, the fundamentals of scientific investigation were laid down. Philosophy assumed great heights and justice was explored to the core. These great achievements that contributed significantly to the identification of the essentials of world civilisation were, to a very great extent, the

outcome of the application of the rule of law. In fact, law was known in Athens as "Despot Law" (Sovereign law), proclaiming the sovereignty of the law as the ultimate authority of the state. In the modern era, the functioning of a number of states is based on the rule of law, attuned, in many respects, to the principles of justice.

88. On the international plane, peace is still elliptical with power often substituting justice as the dominant force. The interdependence of states due to the globalisation of the affairs of the world requires the acknowledgment of the principles of peace as the guiding force in the conduct of the affairs of nations. Here too, the political nature of man, to use again Aristotelian terminology, must prevail over the zoic element in humanity. Uncontrolled passion for dominance with the material benefits it brings, is what bedevils human affairs on the international plane. The UN has failed, so far, to bring about harmonious coexistence of nations founded on justice.

CHAPTER NINE

JUSTICE IN DAILY LIFE

89. Man is a many sided being. Each person is a distinct and unique entity. Nevertheless humans share instincts, including the instinct of reproduction, contributing to the regeneration of mankind. Also, they share intellectual capacities enabling them to judge, evaluate and pioneer. Reason is the common denominator. The pursuit of happiness is, again, a common characteristic of man. Happiness does give pleasure, but pleasure is not coincident with happiness. The pursuit of pleasure is often an expression of passion which if left uncontrolled may become destructive.

90. Sex is a source of ecstatic pleasure. With the advent and spread of contraceptive devices and relaxation of moral strictures, sexual conduct is primarily pursued for its own sake, as a medium of self-satisfaction. A sense of conquest is present. Many advocate that the male sex is polygamous whereas the female sex is monogamous. This notion developed because of the traditional mastery of men over women. There is no reason to support this proposition or that the two sexes are instinctively oriented in different directions. Of course, engagement in sexual intercourse without the use of contraceptives may have different consequences for men and women. Fear of pregnancy was, in days past, a prohibitory factor for women engaging in sexual activity. Marriage binds people together, usually accompanied by religious or civil marital vows or commitments aiming to tie the couple to one another, not only as the parents of children to come, but also to bind one another sexually prohibiting extramarital sexual affairs.

91. Freedom of movement cannot be curtailed. Also, breaching one's word of commitment to a fellow human being enters the equation of fidelity, of vital importance in human relations. Trust, amongst one another is of great consequence to coexistence of human beings. It is a factor of salient importance in the transaction of human affairs. Hence, the law attaches validity to contracts freely entered into.

92. Freedom of contract is an acknowledged human right which is likely to draw civil consequences in the commercial and marital areas including divorce. In light of the above, while adultery cannot be criminalised, being

the right of every individual to engage in a sexual act with a consenting counterpart, it is not unjust to attach civil consequences to marital infidelity, in the same way that consequences are attached to breach of one's agreement.

93. The pursuit and acquisition of wealth is, by and large, an instinctive tendency of man. The cause can be traced to man's insecurity about the future, on the one hand and man's wish to acquire power through his/her riches on the other. Plutocracy, as earlier explained, has been identified as a system of government with a historic background. Wealth on the other hand, must never be allowed to act as a catalyst of the human rights of others. Taxation is wholly acceptable as a means of bringing about an equilibrium in societal order, a process ensuring enjoyment of human rights by every person.

94. The pursuit of glory ("doxa" – δόξα in Greek) is another tendency of man that must be noticed and explored. An ancient Greek epigram says that "riches have been hated by many but glory by none". Honouring persons who contribute significantly in the field of science or the humanities is, as Plato said, the duty of society. On the other hand, pursuit of glory by an individual for its own sake cannot be divorced from vanity that often leads people to do things in which they do not believe, just to attract attention, hence, the word "vainglory". Knowledge is apt to shelter one from vanity.

95. In their daily contact with other human beings, a wise guide is: "don't do to others what you would not like them to do to yourself". To this, one may add: commitment to truth as the only just basis in human exchanges is mutually beneficial.

96. Human rights chart, to a great extent, the element of propriety in human relations. They define the just course of human conduct in many areas of its manifestation.

97. Disagreement about intellectual or practical matters should never be a source of enmity or steer antagonism but provide ground for investigation. Dialogue is a process of enrichment of knowledge through argument and disputation. Dialogue derives from the Greek word "dialogos" (*διάλογος*) and constitutes the foundation word of dialectics, signifying the process of discerning the validity of a proposition through the dialectical process. One must read Heraclitus (*Ηράκλητος*) to understand the significance of dialectics.

98. Modesty must be cultivated for the benefit of man and society. It frees man from egocentricity and opens ways and avenues to the world and knowledge. It helps grasp what is common in human beings and the cultivation of fellowship. Respect for others is an incident of modesty. In every day action, the guiding principle ought to be not to perceive one's being as standing above fellow human beings. Inequalities in mental capacity, physical strength, appearance and wealth should never be allowed to raise a wall of separation between people, upon reflection that the path of life is common to all.

CHAPTER TEN

JUSTICE AND POLITICS

99. Politics, a Greek word, denotes rival propositions and programmes for the governance of the polis, the city, adapted in modern times to corresponding proposals for the rule of the state. External relations have always been a subject of politics. The adaptation of democracy, in its original form and application to a representative system of government makes politics all the more consequential as the citizenry no longer has a voice at the seat of government and decisions affecting them. The assembly of the state constituted by the totality of citizenry has no direct say in the affairs of the state save, indirectly, through their representatives at the seats of government. Democracy demands that the assembly of people are true to their commitments to those they represent. Elenctic machinery in this respect is rarely present.

100. Nowadays, political parties dominate the political scene seeking power through their nominated representatives at the centres of government. They propound policies often emanating from political doctrines respecting what is perceived to be in the interests of the country. Consequently, election of individual representatives reflects, primarily, adherence to or adoption of the party programme and, less so, choice, of a person as their spokesman in authoritative positions. Of course we are referring to countries adhering to democratic rule. In monocratic or dictatorial regimes, if the two can be distinguished, the public is institutionally kept distant from the ruling centre.

In presidential systems of government the electorate choses separately the legislative and executive powers of the state. Certain decisions or proposals of the executive of a non-legislative character are subject to approval by the legislative body. The doctrine of separation of powers gained prominence in the modern era in light of the different mission of the executive and legislative authorities of the state; that is their separateness and the need to sustain symmetry in the transaction of public affairs. Although the legislature lays down the rules of governance, within the framework of the constitutional order their execution is the responsibility of the executive branch of the state.

101. The realm of the executive is nowadays dominated by economic considerations, financial management and foreign relations, in parallel. It is encouraging that commitment to human rights has led increasingly to the setting up of judicial or quasi-judicial bodies to monitor the functioning of governmental authorities with power to remedy injudicious decisions by reference to law and the rules of sound administration.

102. As a rule, economic policies are fashioned to what is proclaimed to be beneficial for the population as a whole. Class politics, as such, are increasingly played down. Justice to the community as a whole is propounded as the guiding principle in the running of the state. Rarely are the dictates of justice dialectically identified or their philosophical background explored. Remnants of the adherents to the philosophy of soviet style communism retained commitment to programmes that favour the working force, notwithstanding virtual impossibility of identifying this class amongst the working population of the country. Bank management, for instance, forms part of the working force despite their critical role over conditions of the life of the public. Although not the owners of the business, they rank as bosses in the ordinary use of the word.

103. Foreign policy is premised on the interests and obligations of a country as a singular entity. Here, more than in any aspect of government policies, ephemeral, as opposed to long-term, interests of the country, is the decisive force in decision-making. What pays today, irrespective of the long-term shapes, as a rule, state policy. This is my reading of history. Justice is rarely the guide in framing foreign policies.

The United Nations mandated with the mission to ensure peace in world affairs, acknowledge to the permanent members of the Security Council, in a way, the Executive of the organisation, the power to veto decisions of the fifteen-membered body. The conferment of such power evinces disinclination on the part of the strong and powerful nations, to relinquish authority collectively and individually over fellow members of the United Nations. Many support that the principal considerations that count for super-powers, a term often used, in framing their course of action, are their interests extending worldwide and their service. The examples, revealing double standards on the part of powerful states are too many to recount. While they proclaim democracy and the rule of law at home, they often come to terms with dictatorial and oppressive regimes abroad. They may even aid the displacement of a democratic government of a foreign country if their perceived interests so warrant. As it did happen in 1953, with the overthrow of the democratic government of Dr Mosaddegh, after the nationalisation of the Anglo-Iranian petroleum company. The military occupation of Suez by the British and French armies in 1956 after the nationalisation by the Egyptian government of the Suez Canal is yet another example of the wiliness of powerful nations. The invasion in 1979 and sequential domination of Afghanistan by the Soviet Union is a striking example of military intervention by a superpower in a smaller and weaker nation. The brutal suppression by the Soviet Union of popular uprisings in Hungary in 1956 and Czechoslovakia in 1958, countries within their sphere of influence, demonstrate the implications of the rule of power as opposed to the rule of law. The endless imprisonment of suspected terrorists at Guantanamo, an American base in Cuba, has become a notorious story, a true insult to the dictates of justice. Indifference of powerful nations to injustice around the world is another stigma of modern times. The Turkish invasion and sequential occupation of a large part of Cyprus in 1974 and displacement therefrom of the vast majority of its population, Greek, ethnic cleansing at its worst and settlement of the area by Turks from Turkey, is another tragic story. That crimes against humanity, the worst form of injustice, are suffered for so long, is a sad indication of the fate of small countries on the one hand and indifference of the world to blatant injustice on the other.

Realpolitik as opposed to humanitarian rule is what epitomises injustice in worldly affairs.

104. Globalisation of finance and, correspondingly, increase of the influence of professional investors has, to an extent, taken finance out of the hands of government, turning economic planning by ordinary people into an uncertain venture. Consequently, the individual and his/her savings at the stock exchange and the value of their portofolio is exposed to the plans and whims of speculators. Justice in the sense of protection of man within the context of the community requires the adoption of measures and mechanisms shielding the person from such perils. It has been written that had it not been for the world depression of 1929 that continued for a few years, rendering millions of Germans unemployed, the Nazi party would never have come to power in Germany. They point out that in the elections of 1928 the votes secured by that party appeared to be declining, whereas in the elections held at the end of 1931-1932 the Nazi party gained more votes and sequentially more seats in parliament than any other party, opening thereby the way for its ascent to power.

105. Improved means of transport have made contact between people across the world easier, expanding the channels of communication.

The Internet too, has likewise opened avenues of communication across the globe. These developments are conducive to removing barriers that keep people apart, improve mutual understanding and pave the way for humanity treading a common path. The needs of humanity in its natural environment are better served through dialogue and exchange of information enhancing thereby the potential of man through realisation, inter alia, that division of humanity is counterproductive. Combination of human forces makes life easier and serves present and long-term interests of the individual and humanity in its entirety, promoting thereby the ends of justice. Regional associations of states mark the way forward.

106. Taxation and social security are principal aspects of economic policies. Amenity to acquire wealth is no longer a privilege of the few. Notwithstanding inequalities, it is within the reach of everyone to share in communal wealth. Sharing in this respect is an aim proclaimed by nearly every party in democratic societies. The predominant route to secure it is through taxation on the one hand and social security on the other. Taxation must be progressive, requiring contribution according to means without eradicating self-interest as an agent of the productive forces. Social security aims to provide those in need with the necessaries to sustain life with dignity and keep alive the creative forces of man. Health and housing are vital components of social security. So are programmes for the education and training of the unemployed to meet the ever-changing needs of modern societies. Ensuring harmonious co-existence in society is a principal goal of justice.

107. The expansion of the field of central government and improved means of secreting and hiding their actions, makes it all the more necessary to introduce and/or extend institutional elenctic measures to ensure that government operates within the realm of the law and in accordance with the principles of fair administration. This is imperative for the protection of the state from misdoing and upholding the rights of man. The civil service has grown in size and the range of its operations augmented. Surveillance of their action is needed in the interest of the rule of law. Corruption in the management of the affairs of the state, including nepotism is a diachronic phenomenon, not to be suffered. Meritocracy must be upheld at all times and at all costs and every species of bribery combatted. Government action must be monitored by independent authorities and remedied where necessary. This task should be entrusted

to administrative courts or comparable judicial institutions with a wide-ranging mandate to remedy injustice in the domain of public administration. The principles of fair trial, universally acknowledged, as the process through which justice should be ministered, must define the procedural framework of the conduct of the proceedings. A basic safeguard in this and other respects to stem maladministration, lies in the establishment of an independent and autonomous prosecutorial authority; a watchdog of the rule of law.

108. Knowledge of the law was a requisite of democracy at its inception and early practice. Democracy itself was regarded as the offspring of the law giving expression to fundamental norms of justice. Modern societies are inundated with volumes of legislation, rules and regulations. Ways must be found and means employed to inform the public in plain language of the various aspects of the law, especially principles of law of universal application. As a rule, people are presumed to know the law, an unrealistic presumption given the magnitude and implications of the law in force. Public sources of information must be made available, enabling the public to gain knowledge of the various aspects of it and the individual to plan his/her life and affairs with the necessary certainty. One could legitimately argue that justice and the law should be included in the curriculum of both elementary and secondary education. Law is what fastens people together and lays the ground for sound decisions by the state and the individual.

109. The mandate of the executive and legislative powers of the state ranges, as a rule, between four to five years. The programme of government and the party or parties that support it, is delineated by foreseeable events at the time of gaining their mandate to rule. Not infrequently, unforeseeable, at the time of the election, serious situations and events occur requiring decision-making. This is not uncommon especially in relation to foreign affairs, an example being the decision by the United States of America and the United Kingdom to wage war against Iraq, a sad affair plunging the country into a bloody war on fake grounds. Commitment to democracy would require the holding of a plebiscite in order to solicit the position of the electorate on the matter. That is the recipe for democratic legitimation in addressing serious issues affecting the public not touched upon at the time of election. This is the just course affording the electorate the opportunity to express its view on vital issues concerning the life of the community and the individual.

110. Media of mass communication informing of unfolding events are primarily the means through which the public gains knowledge of what goes on at home and abroad. Newspapers, periodicals and television, commentaries on the emerging scene, provide room for the evaluation of governmental action, its implications and events portraying the political scene. True reporting and unbiased commentation, constitute a true service to the country and humanity. On the other hand, untrue, coloured or glossed account of events and misleading commentaries constitute a disservice to the public, apt to generate falsehood often associated with an intention to influence the public to support a cause favoured by the transmitters. The same can occur if the importance of an event is underrated or exaggerated.

It is of the first importance for society to establish mechanisms for overseeing the process followed by mass media with a view to mitigating deviation from true and accurate reporting through misrepresentation of facts. Plunging society into falsehood is damaging to the individual and the community as a whole. Truth is the guide to the identification of the demands of justice.

Many mass media are controlled by private individuals. Also, there are state corporations running radio and television stations. In both cases, need arises for independent monitoring with a view to sustaining true reporting and representation of events. Mechanism must be put in place to serve this cause.

One cannot but notice that, to a noticeable extent, television has replaced the book as the companion of individuals in their spare time. Of course, man is free to devote his time at his choice. Nonetheless, it is beneficial that measures should be taken to encourage the display on television of educational, as well as informative programmes for the benefit of the audience.

111. Local government has an important role to play in the management of the affairs of the locality and rendering humanitarian services to the people within its boundaries. Party politics hold a significant part in the election of the mayor and councillors of a municipality but not as thorough as in general elections. Local personalities do count by reference to services rendered to the community. Because of the numerical limitation of the local electorate, room is provided for the direct participation of the population in the area of decision making on vital issues such as planning policies and providing necessary support for those in need. This

can be achieved in public assemblies at various areas of the municipality. Such a process would inevitably sustain and cultivate the sense of responsibility of the public in matters of direct interest to them. Involvement of the public in decision-making is propitious to the cultivation of one's sense of responsibility. There are many who support extension of the mandate of local authorities for two reasons; firstly, to relieve congestion in central government quarters and secondly, to enhance direct participation of the public in matters vitally affecting their life.

112. Politics constitute the dialectics of the running of society. The measure of judging the merits of the various propositions is the good of society, as an inseverable part of humanity. Unbiased knowledge is what paves the road to justice. Participation of the individual in public affairs is a safeguard against alienation of humans from communal affairs and the rights of man as a distinct part of the whole. Democratic rule is the only system of government that recognises the will of the public as the dominant force in society, hence the great value of education as the route to knowledge on the one hand, and on the other, protection from misery that undermines the dignity of man and neutralises free will.

PART II

THE JUDICIARY

CHAPTER ELEVEN

OBJECT AND PURPOSE

113. The Judiciary is the guardian of justice. It is the body entrusted with the enforcement of the law and the sustenance of what befits justice. In societies functioning under the rule of law, it is the ultimate authority to determine what is permissible or impermissible, acceptable or unacceptable and generally what is right or wrong.

114. Most religions postulate the ministration of justice as a Godly affair, casting God as the ultimate Judge of human deeds, thoughts and actions, dispensing punishment or rewards, accordingly. In life, the Judge is the dispenser of justice through a system of reinstatement of an injured party and punishment of ill-doers. The determination of the propriety of governmental and administrative action is another important branch of justice designed to ensure that the authorities operate within the parameters of the law and the margins of their authority, with due regard to the rights of man.

115. The incorporation of the values and ideals of justice into law has a long history, not alien to that of democracy as earlier noticed. Democracy was identified and adopted as a system of government in ancient Ionia, going by the name of Isonomy, that is equality before the law and every institution of the state. Subsequently, it was renamed "Democracy" in Athens, that is, rule by the people, founded on three pillars: isonomy, isopolity and isocracy; in other words, it was adopted as the system of government best fitting just rule. In the modern era, the combination of the two backbones of the system, notably rule under the law founded on principles of justice and majority rule, takes the form of constitutionalism, that is, superior law encoding the fundamentals of justice within which democratic rule should operate.

116. The United States Declaration of Independence and sequentially, the American Constitution, incorporated fundamental norms of justice subject to which the American state would function in many spheres of life. It incorporated first and foremost fundamental and inalienable norms of human rights and marked the path of governance according to law. The triad of the French Revolution *liberté-égalité–fraternité* was a source

of inspiration aimed to free man from the shackles of constraint. Nowadays, the protection of human rights, especially after the Universal Declaration of Human Rights of 1948, is a dominant field of constitutionalism. The very notion of constitutional order implies and inevitably imports the creation and establishment of a constitutional court empowered with authority to determine whether governmental or legislative institutional action is compatible with the constitution and if not, to disown the law, executive or administrative action. Here too, the Judiciary is trusted as the guardian of constitutional order. The supremacy of the law is identified with the supremacy of justice inasmuch as the basic law is meant to incorporate fundamental notions of justice.

117. From old, the judiciary was perceived as a separate estate, distinct from the Executive and Legislative branches of government. The separation of powers of the state is primarily designed to institutionalise the independence and impartiality of the judiciary from every other source of authority. The principal functions of the judiciary may be identified as follows:

i) Interpretation of the law. Several ways of interpretation have found favour. First and foremost the grammatical interpretation, that is, the interpretation of the text of the law by reference to the wording used to give expression to the desired ends.
ii) Purposive or teleological interpretation, giving prominence in the interpretative process to the objects the law is intended to promote. The term teleological, a word emanating from Greek, correlates interpretation to the ends the legislation is intended to serve.

a) A combination of the two, that is, grammatical and purposive interpretation, may provide a solid guide to the interpretation of the law. The language used, signifies the immediate object in the context of the general aims of the legislation. This means that there is no warrant for departing from the text of the law but there is room for so doing, where the wording of legislation is either obscure or inconclusive, whereupon resort may be had to the wider aims of the law in order to discern the meaning of the relevant provision.

b) Where statutory and customary law find application side by side, as in England and countries adhering to the common law system, the identification of principles of customary law and the range of their application is in the domain of the judiciary. Several rules have been developed to regulate the relationship between statutory and customary law and the principles by reference to which, a common law rule can be overrun or overtaken by a statute. The principal one is that the legislature is presumed to know the common law and consequently it can only be credited with an intention to abolish it when it says so explicitly.

118. The system of separation of powers is premised on the principle that no state authority can be a judge in its own cause. Aristotle first, spoke of the necessity to keep the powers of the state separate from one another in order to ensure symmetry in the governance of the *polis*.

119. In the modern era, Montesquieu addressed the principle of separation of powers in his work "The Spirit of the Law", giving prominence in this connection to the independence of the English judiciary, notwithstanding the fact that the three powers of the English state were not, and to an extent they are still not, formally separated.

120. Nowadays a formal separation of the powers of the state is regarded as an inseverable element of the doctrine. The compass of each of the three authorities of the state is separated, ensuring to each power autonomy in its sphere of authority. The field of the judiciary lies in the identification of the law, its interpretation and enforcement in the case before it, coupled with such authority as necessary to give effect to its decisions.

CHAPTER TWELVE

THE MISSION OF THE JUDICIARY

121. The principal functions of the judiciary are:

1. The resolution of disputes of every kind between persons, singly or as part of corporate entities and disputes between citizens and the state
2. Passing judgment on the legitimacy of legislation and action of the executive and administrative authorities. In some countries, power is acknowledged to the judiciary to pronounce on the constitutionality of a law pre-emptively, that is, before promulgation.
3. Administration of criminal law, meting out punishment to those found guilty of committing a crime

122. The undercurrent of judicial action is that justice be done. Consequently, the whole process of applying the law should be subject to the fundamental principles of justice incorporated in the basic law. In England there is no written constitution; nonetheless, from early times, as noted in the previous chapter, equity filled the gap to an extent by empowering the judiciary to rule out inequitable action. Hence the principle that, where equity and the common law are in conflict, the former shall prevail. Also, note must be taken of the Magna Carta of 1215 and the Bill of Rights of 1689 giving expression to a number of inalienable rights of man.

123. In the process of ministering justice, the judiciary must, in the first place, define the subject-matter of the conflict or dispute, and generally the issues before it. The fact- finding process, that is, the determination of the true facts bearing on the issues before the court, is an important facet of judicial action. Only evidence relevant to the subject-matter of the proceedings is admissible. Even relevant evidence may, on occasion, be rejected either on account of lack of probative value or its emanation from a polluted source. The rules governing the admissibility of evidence are the guide to the admission or exclusion of evidence and to an extent, its evaluation.

124. Species of evidence may, because of the delicacy of the context in which they emerge, be subject to corroboration from an independent source before its acceptance as a condition of its creditworthiness.

125. Eliciting the law and applying it to the facts of the case, is a significant aspect of judgment writing. Reasoning a judgment is a basic attribute of a fair trial. It is a hedge against arbitrariness on the part of the judiciary and a form of accountability of the exercise of judicial power. Defining the precise meaning and import of the law is part of the process of judgment writing, and, where the system of binding precedent is followed, the determination of its compatibility with the judicial diachronic perspective of jurisprudence is another aspect of it.

126. The remedies available to the judiciary are also a sequential factor in the administration of justice. They must be such as to enable the Court to do justice in the case before it. The acknowledgment of rights, if that is the only subject in dispute, is given expression to by a declaration. An injunction is a means to prohibit repetition of conduct violative of the rights of the claimant. As a rule, power is conferred on the court, to issue not only final but interlocutory injunctions too. The aim, in the latter case is to prevent irreparable injury and damage such as would make it impossible, or very difficult to do justice at the end of the case. In a way, it is a means of preserving the status-quo. Security must be given by the plaintiff to compensate or restore the rights of the defendant, the subject of an interim injunction, where the motion is ultimately dismissed. A final injunction as the word suggests is a permanent prohibition of the defendant from engaging in illegal or impermissible action.

127. Damages are meant to recompense and compensate for loss and injury inflicted on the plaintiff and foreseeably expected to be suffered in the future. Moreover, residual power is acknowledged to the Court in some jurisdictions to award, in addition to pecuniary, what are characterised as moral or equitable damages, that is, non-pecuniary damages resulting from the contemptuous conduct of the defendant. For similar reasons, aggravated damages or even exemplary damages may be awarded to the injured claimant amounting to the use of the civil process as a means of punishment for gravely offensive conduct on the part of the defendant. A remedy available in land disputes is specific performance, that is, an order directing the defendant to transfer immovable property to the claimant. Failure to comply exposes the defaulter to contempt of court. The award of costs is another remedy available to the Court.

The discretion of the civil court in this area is usually exercised by reference to the outcome of the case and the conduct of the parties to the proceedings.

128. The family court is another branch of the civil process, vested with jurisdiction to dissolve marriages, make orders for the custody of children as well as their maintenance. Jurisdiction also lies with family courts to settle financial matters between spouses and issue injunctions where a member of the couple evinces destructive tendencies towards the family or its cohesion. New branches of the judiciary emerged in modern times endowed with jurisdiction to address special areas of the law such as legislation concerning employment, industrial disputes, rent control and other distinct areas of human enterprise and action.

CHAPTER THIRTEEN

CRIMINAL LAW

129. Criminal law, deriving from customary and statutory law, defines criminal conduct and makes provision for the punishment of offenders. According to the jurisprudence of the European Court of Human Rights, the adversarial system is best suited to a criminal trial. The presumption of innocence makes that inevitable, requiring the accuser to prove the opposite. With the passage of time, measures of punishment have become less harsh, especially with the impact of human rights upon the complexion of the law. It need only be reminded that in the year 1800, 160 crimes carried the death penalty in England. Deportation was another measure of punishment not infrequently resorted to, a measure that historically helped the British colonise some of their dominions.

130. With rare exceptions, imprisonment is nowadays the severest form of punishment, designed as a retributory measure and a reformative one. A suspended sentence of imprisonment is a relatively new method of treatment of offenders, allowing the suspension of imprisonment on terms designed to keep the offender away from committing another crime within a specified period of time. The right to suspend is confined to relatively short terms of imprisonment below two or three years. If the accused commits no crime within the specified period he/she is absolved of the obligation to serve the sentence of imprisonment. On the contrary, if a crime is committed, the sentence may be activated and the prisoner, in addition, can be sentenced for the new offence. So, the convict is liable to be imprisoned, both for the original and the new crime.

131. A confiscation order is primarily meant to deprive the offender of the fruits and benefits acquired through the commission of the crime. A compensation order is another way of restoring the victim to the position he/she would have been, had the individual not been the victim of the conduct the subject-matter of the crime. It must be noticed that, in criminal proceedings, a compensation order is rarely made and then, only with the agreement of victim and offender. The criminal court is not the appropriate forum for the assessment and award of damages.

Recognisance to keep the law for a specified period of time for minor offences may be had recourse to binding the offender to keep the law within a specified period of time; failing which, the convicted person forfeits the recognisance and becomes liable to be punished for the new violation of criminal law. Recognisance to come up for judgment exposes the accused, in addition to forfeiture of his recognisance, to be punished for the crime earlier committed. Probation, that is, supervision of the convict, usually by the welfare authorities, often for a period of two or three years, is another form of treatment, resorted to primarily in the case of minors and young offenders. It is primarily a corrective measure to combat antisocial behaviour on the part of the offender.

132. The imposition of a duty to do social work for a period of time is a new expedient of reformative justice and a form of atonement for the crime committed, which the court may order. In crimes emanating from the addiction of the offender to prohibited substances, an order may be made, that the convict does submit to medical care, in addition to imprisonment or as a substitute for it. This form of treatment may be had recourse to, where, owing to the pressure of addiction, the convict is unable to give up the distractive habit without medical help.

133. Juvenile Courts are a branch of the judiciary trusted with jurisdiction over offences committed by minors. Probation and other forms of supervision is the usual treatment for minor offenders. The reform school is another mode of punishment of minors guilty of serious crime. Imprisonment is not ruled out if they are above a certain age, usually 14 or 15, although regarded as a measure of last resort.

CHAPTER FOURTEEN

REVISIONAL JURISDICTION

134. Administrative Courts are the branch of the Judiciary invested with jurisdiction to determine the validity of acts, decisions and omissions of the Administration, that is, the layer of the Executive that determines rights and obligations of the individual. Sound administration, notably the right exercise of powers vested in state authorities, is one of the hallmarks of government under the law. The object of judicial review is to pronounce on the validity of an act, decision or omission, wherefrom rights emerge, obligations are imposed or the discharge of duties is neglected.

135. Omission to act where a duty to do so is imposed upon the Administration, may be the subject of judicial review in order to test the legality of inaction and if wanting to order the Administration to do what it ought to have done. In reviewing administrative acts, the Judiciary will not step into the shoes of the Administration nor will it test their validity by what the Court regards as the right decision. The Administration may take, within the context of the law, any decision reasonably open to it. The review is confined to the legality of the action, that is, whether the administration operated within the bounds of the law and in accordance with the tenets of sound administration. It is the duty of the Administration, in arriving at a decision or taking action, to search for and identify the relevant facts, evaluate them by reference to the norms of proper administration and reason its decision, explaining the process leading to it and the reasons warranting it.

136. So long as a decision was reasonably open to the Administration, the court will not interfere with it. The object of the exercise is to test whether the Administration acted within the prescients of the law with due regard to the principles of sound administration. The aim of judicial review is not to supplant the Administration but to ensure that it operates within the parameters of the law with a view to promoting its objectives. In the case of omissions, the object is to determine whether a duty to act is imposed by law on the Administration, and, if so, whether it failed to carry it out, in which case, the omission will be declared invalid, followed by an order commanding the Administration to do what it ought to have done.

CHAPTER FIFTEEN

CONSTITUTIONAL JURISDICTION

137. Where a country has a constitution as its supreme or basic law, corresponding jurisdiction is vested in the judiciary to determine the constitutionality of laws, rules and regulations emanating from the legislative and executive branches of government. Pre-emptive constitutional control is acknowledged in some countries, that is, power to determine *a priori* whether the impugned law, rule or regulation, violates, in one or more respects, the constitution.

Constitutional jurisdiction embraces every aspect of constitutional order. The constitutionality of a law may be referred to the court by the president or any other specified authority of the state before its promulgation. Otherwise, jurisdiction should vest in the judiciary to determine the constitutionality of any law whenever necessary for the resolution of the subject-matter of the proceedings.

138. Constitutional jurisdiction is ordinarily conferred on a distinct branch of the judiciary, namely to a constitutional court. Issues of constitutionality arising in any other branch of the judiciary are, as a rule, referred to the constitutional court for resolution. A law or sections of it declared unconstitutional are deemed to be invalid *ab initio*, from the date of their promulgation, whereas, in the case of pre-emptive constitutional control, the impugned legislation is tested before it comes into force. It must be mentioned that principles of customary law may be declared unconstitutional if offensive to one or more relevant provisions of the constitution.

Fundamental norms of justice are, as a rule, incorporated in a supreme law, usually the constitution, as well as the parameters of authority of the various governmental seats of power. Amenity to change, annul or amend the provisions of the constitution vests in the legislative assembly requiring, as a rule, an increased majority, two thirds or three quarters of its members, or, in an assembly of representatives specially elected, to deal with the matter or by plebiscite.

CHAPTER SIXTEEN

JUDGES

139. A judge is one who ministers justice. The word derives from the same root as the word justice notably from the latin term justitia (judge – judic). The two words, justice and judge, have, as noted, a common origin, underlying the mission of a judge to dispense justice. A judge personifies justice in its administration.

140. Knowledge of the law is a vital qualification for the appointment or election of a candidate to a judicial position. The basic qualifications for judicial appointment are ordinarily specified in the constitution and detailed or itemised in a law. In some systems, especially common law systems, practical experience as a lawyer for a minimum period of years is an indispensable qualification. It provides first hand evidence of the commitment of a lawyer to the ends of justice. In other countries, graduation of a legally qualified person from a school tutoring students in the discharge of judicial duties, is postulated as a necessary qualification for appointment. High moral standing is another qualification signifying righteous conduct in one's life, a person of integrity.

141. Hereinbefore we identified the formal qualifications normally required for appointment to a judicial position. The list is not exhaustive. Knowledge of the history, especially the history of legal evolution, the principles of law, their correlation to the background of their adoption and application in the ever-changing stratum of life is also essential. Law is a living organism, the subject of many philosophical works, the discipline that explores the inner core of the forces of life with a view to deciphering transcendental or eternal principles of justice. Justice in its various manifestations is a basic theme of philosophy. Dialectics, an important discipline, enabling through contrast of opposites and forces that move either way the discernment of the substance of things on the one hand and the application of a principle in the various walks of life on the other, is highly relevant to the ascertainment of the essence, the identification of the core of an issue by the juxtaposition of counter propositions bearing on a subject.

142. Above all, a judge must free himself from prejudice inculcated by cultural and social forces and emotional traits, a key element in the sustenance of the neutrality of a judge at all times and in all circumstances. It is expected of a judge to administer justice impersonally and dispassionately in the complex world.

143. To enable the judge to carry out the judicial mission, he/she must be endowed with residual power to ensure that justice is done. We are referring, not to a power vesting in the judiciary authority to do what the holder of the office perceives as right, but to a recognised jurisdiction to remedy injustice in the given circumstances of a case from the strict application or elliptic provisions of the law. The object is not to by-pass the law but to apply it in a spirit and manner befitting justice. This is a corrective process that found application in English law by the evolution of the principles of equity. Maxims of equity provide apt examples of fundamental notions of justice.

"Whoever seeks equity, must come to court with clean hands", in other words, proceedings must serve a legitimate purpose, not be flawed by ulterior motives. *"Equality is equity"*;
"Whoever seeks equity must himself conform to the principles of equity".
"No wrong can be suffered without a remedy", emphasising the need for mechanism to redress injustice.

144. Equity developed specific remedies associated with fidelity in the transaction of human affairs and the confidence that should characterise the private domain of life. Equitable estoppel, as well as proprietory estoppel, are remedies designed to prevent injustice by stopping the ill-doer from benefitting from breach of his/her word to the detriment of the promisee. Breach of confidence is another area where equitable jurisdiction may be assumed to stop the misdeed and remedy its breach. In modern times, fundamental tenets of justice are incorporated in the constitution, charting the parametres of the administration of justice.

CHAPTER SEVENTEEN

FAIR TRIAL

145. Assurance of a fair trial is a fundamental human right, the emblem of restorative justice. A fair trial constitutes a fundamental right of man and correspondingly, a principal duty of the State to secure in all circumstances. No deviation or shortfall of a fair trial should be countenanced. The norms of a fair trial are fashioned to the needs of justice. It is the inexhaustible duty of the Court to do justice according to the norms of a fair trial. In its absence, freedom of man is muted and man's hypostasis undermined. A fair trial can appropriately be labelled as the bedrock of human rights.

CHAPTER EIGHTEEN

THE REQUISITES OF A FAIR TRIAL

146. The requisites of a fair trial can be identified as follows: First and foremost, the independence and impartiality of the Court. The two concepts are interrelated. Independence denotes free spirit, freedom from every source of interest and influence, social, financial and political. A judge must act like one not only in court, but outside it too. The independence of a judge must be demonstrable 24 hours a day.

147. Impartiality imports neutrality in every material respect, distance from the conflict unfolding before the Court, subjectively and objectively demonstrable. Out of court associations, statements and conduct apt to blur one's impartiality may disqualify him/her on objective grounds. The test is whether a reasonable person acquainted with the facts of the case may discern a real possibility of lack of impartiality. A judge must refrain from joining closed societies, or societies of eclectic status and certainly a judge must keep distant from political parties and generally the political scene. Belonging to a party signifies espousal of its objects and purposes. The principle of separation of powers dictates that a judge should distance himself from the domain of the Executive and Legislative branches of government as well as their forerunners, the parties that voted for them.

A key question is whether party members should be disqualified from appointment to the bench, until they distance themselves from politics for a sufficiently long interval of time to objectively dissociate themselves from the political association to which they belonged. I subscribe to this view because association with a party colours both the independence and impartiality of a judge. Under any circumstances, a person appointed to the judiciary must sever links from every political, or eclectic association, or group of persons that may colour his/her outlook in any direction.

148. The election of judges raises serious questions about the attributes of their independence and impartiality. The election of a judge may be tied to the support of a party. If so, the independence of a judge objectively evaluated from sources of influence is forfeited *ab initio* and his/her impartiality becomes questionable. The election of a judge on the basis of

a preferred interpretation of legislation or the promotion of a legal cause likewise exposes the judge to forfeiture of the credentials of independence and impartiality. The politicisation of the judiciary is anathema to justice. Only a candidate who seeks election by reference to his/her commitment to the ends of justice retains, in the eyes of the public, the attributes of independence and impartiality.

CHAPTER NINETEEN

SELECTION OF JUDGES

149. This is perhaps the most delicate issue in any country committed to the rule of law. In the past, political powers played a significant, if not a decisive role in the choice of a judge, especially judges of the Superior Courts. The adoption of human rights as a superior legal norm, particularly the independence and impartiality of the judiciary as the inalienable right of man and commitment to the principle of separation of powers, has brought home that the two political powers of the state, the Executive and the Legislature should have no say and should take no part in the selection and appointment of judges.

150 As earlier noted, the concept of democracy has been *ab initio* associated with the rule of law. In Ancient Athens, the selection of jurors was made by lot as a safeguard against any form of partiality.

The professional judiciary, being in many cases, judges of law and fact trusted to administer justice perennially, must at all times maintain the credentials of independence and impartiality. I have often seen it written that the judiciary of such and such a period was liberal, progressive, conservative, even reactionary by reference to the overlords who appointed them. The most effective way to safeguard the independence and impartiality of the professional judiciary, I say professional because jurors too, may participate in the process of judgment rendering, is to entrust the power of appointment and promotion of judges to a Council of Judicature composed primarily of judges and possibly others concerned with the administration of justice such as eminent jurists. The process of selection must be open and the decision duly reasoned. Judges of all grades in the judicial hierarchy should receive the same salary in recognition of the fact that they render services of equal value to the community. First instance, appellate and superior courts, have the same mission, to do justice at the different levels of the judicial hierarchy. Equality of salaries would acknowledge this reality. It is an edict of justice that terms and conditions of service of judges should not be altered to their disadvantage after appointment. This is a safeguard of their independence. The right to retire at any time the judge chooses to must likewise be safeguarded as a necessary incident of the independence of the judiciary and freedom from any source of pressure. Disciplinary proceedings against judges for misconduct should be assigned to a judicial disciplinary board. Such proceedings should be of a judicial nature attuned to the norms of a fair trial.

CHAPTER TWENTY

INTERNATIONAL JUDICIARY

151. The international judiciary is an institution of the 20th century. Suggestions and motions for the establishment of international judicial bodies came to the fore in the latter part of the 19th and early years of the 20th century. The statement of the leaders of the *entente cordiale* of 1915 to the effect that Turks who committed crimes against humanity would not go unpunished but would be prosecuted at the end of the war, as justice warranted, was ignored as the interests of the victorious allies appeared to dictate. In fact, the Turks were absolved by the treaty of Lausanne of 1923 for crimes committed, the genocide of the Armenians and other minorities. Amnesty was granted. Amnesty, deriving from the Greek word *αμνηστία* denotes, in its original sense, to be forgotten about.

152. The establishment of the League of Nations after the First World War and the Permanent Court of Justice signaled the first steps for the establishment of organised world order, found on law. The Court was an institution of the League of Nations empowered to resolve disputes between nations. Both the League of Nations and the Permanent Court of Justice collapsed with the militarisation of the resolution of disputes between European and other powers of the world. In the aftermath of the Second World War the United Nations was established as the guardian of peace and the International Court of Justice was invested with jurisdiction to resolve disputes between states and also render opinions to the Security Council, in matters of concern to its sphere of authority.

153. Special criminal tribunals were established to try German and Japanese war criminals of the Second World War, notably the Nuremberg and Tokyo Tribunals. They were ad hoc courts manned by judges emanating from the victorious states. Some have identified these tribunals as victors' courts. This cannot be denied, but neither can it be overlooked that the Nuremberg tribunal, in particular, made a contribution to international criminal law. The expedient of setting up ad hoc international courts has been resorted to recently with a view to bringing to justice persons who committed grave crimes against humanity and war crimes in localised wars. Such are the International Criminal Tribunal for Former

Yugoslavia (1993), the International Criminal Tribunal for Rwanda (1994) and the international mixed courts (composed of international and local judges) of Siera Leone (1996) and Cambodia (2003). The establishment of the International Criminal Court obviates the need for such tribunals for crimes committed after its coming into force.

154. Movements for the establishment of an international criminal court started after the Second World War. The Convention on Genocide of 1948 envisages the possibility of such an occurrence. Motions for the establishment of such a court were intensified at the end of the 1980's and the process gained momentum in 1994 with the establishment of an international conference to address the issue. The conference was concluded in 1998 with the adoption of the Rome Statute for the International Criminal Court. The treaty came into force on the 1st July 2002 after 60 signatories ratified the treaty and the Court became functional soon after. The Court is vested with worldwide jurisdiction to try serious crimes of concern to the international community, namely, genocide, crimes against humanity, war crimes and the crime of aggression. In the case of the latter, jurisdiction may be assumed after 2017 following a resolution of the States Parties to that end.

155. The Rome Statute specifies the qualifications for the election of judges who must derive from all geographical regions of the world. To be elected, a judge must secure at least two thirds of the votes of Member States participating and voting at the election. The Court is an autonomous body vested residually, that is, in the absence of specific provisions on a subject, with such powers as necessary to carry out its mission. A supplementary instrument is the Rules of Procedure and Evidence, regulating the conduct of the proceedings on the one hand and the admissibility of evidence on the other. The Regulations of the Court approved by the Judges of the Court aim to supplement the Rules of Procedure and Evidence with a view to prescribing the conduct of different species of judicial proceedings before the Court. The court has three Divisions, the Pre-Trial, the Trial and the Appeals Division. An appeal lies from specified decisions of the first two layers of the Court to the third. Human rights are duly safeguarded, constituting one of the pillars of the statute. The Vienna Convention on the Law of Treaties provides a comprehensive guide to the interpretation of international treaties and conventions.

156. The Office of the Prosecutor is another authority for which provision is made in the statute, institutionally separated from the judicial side of the Court. The Prosecutor is vested with wide powers including the power to initiate proceedings *proprio motu*.

157. The exercise of the jurisdiction of the Court is subject to the following conditions:

a) the Court can only heed crimes within its jurisdiction committed after the statute came into force, notably the 1st July 2002
b) the crime must have been committed within a member state or by its nationals
c) worldwide jurisdiction is conferred on the Court, in relation to crimes committed anywhere in the world, referred to it by the Security Council of the United Nations.
d) cases may be referred to the Prosecutor for investigation and action by member states or the Security Council. Jurisdiction also vests in the Prosecutor to act in relation to a situation *proprio motu* upon complaint being made to the Prosecutor's Office or information reaching him/her about the commission of crimes within the jurisdiction of the Court
e) the jurisdiction of the Court is complementary and not a substitute for the jurisdiction of member states. Inability or unwillingness of states, signified by diverse acts provides evidence of refusal or inaction, to bring to justice, offenders committing crimes within the jurisdiction of the Court; whereupon the international criminal court may assume jurisdiction.

The International Criminal Court is a landmark in the history of humanity because individuals, wherever they come from or reside, committing crimes within the jurisdiction of the Court, are liable to prosecution in the manner envisaged by the statute. In particular:

a) The Statute stresses that the world community is subject to the same rules in relation to crimes that have scarred humanity
b) the identity of the accused is irrelevant. Everyone, from the head of state downwards is liable to prosecution and conviction. This is a most salutary provision stressing that criminal liability is at all times and in all circumstances personal.

CHAPTER TWENTY-ONE

EXERCISE OF JUDICIAL DUTIES

158. A judge must retain his/her distance and be aloof from the conflict unfolding before the Court. The neutrality of the judge must be evident at every stage of the proceedings. The judge must personify justice in its administration. This, of course, should not prevent him/her from seeking clarification of obscure or hard to comprehend propositions or evidence.

159. What the judge must never do by word or conduct, is to compromise the stance of neutrality. Patience to listen to evidence and arguments advanced, must be cultivated to the utmost, so must cordiality in addressing anyone before the Court. At the same time, the judge must be strict in ensuring that the judicial process follows the course ordained by law. When an issue arises in the course of a hearing, the duty of the judge is to listen to the parties and determine the matter before the court, if possible without more ado. Here comes in, thorough knowledge of the law.

160. Witnesses unable to take the oath or give an affirmation to tell the truth, because of immaturity or mental deficiency, may be allowed to give evidence, provided they possess the capacity to comprehend things generally and distinguish between right and wrong. Persons lying on oath or affirmation are criminally liable for the crime of perjury in separate proceedings. It must be underlined that the mere finding of a judge of believing or disbelieving a witness cannot ground perjury. More is needed, independent evidence revealing the falsity of the testimony.

161. The trial does not open the floodgates for the production of evidence. Evidence to be received must be relevant to the subject-matter of the proceedings and admissible under the rules of evidence. Relevance is a matter of logic. Admissibility is the offspring of the rules of evidence designed to exclude irrelevant evidence, as well as evidence inherently unreliable or deriving from a polluted source such as evidence secured through breach of the human rights of a person. Inadmissible is also evidence of a crime engineered by police authorities with a view to catching the prospective culprit(s).

162. It is wrong to impose a time limit on the duration of the testimony of a witness. Such a course may result in the exclusion of relevant evidence, necessary explanation of it and more than that, create a climate of haste, unpropitious to the ends of justice.

CHAPTER TWENTY-TWO

ADMINISTRATION OF JUSTICE WITHIN A REASONABLE TIME

163. It is a canon of fair trial that justice should be dispensed within a reasonable time, that is, within such time as reason can justify. In criminal cases, time begins to run from the moment investigations start or the suspect is arrested. In civil cases, time begins to run from the institution of a case within the limits of a prescriptive period, if any. It can be argued that unreasonable delay in reporting the commission of a crime is a factor that should count in the determination of the reasonableness of the time within which the proceedings should be concluded. Memory may be dimmed by the lapse of time, a factor not to be overlooked in the assessment of the value and probativeness of evidence.

164. A deliberate long delay to report a crime tends to suggest that the reporter is actuated by ulterior motives. Furthermore, such delay inevitably prolongs the time within which justice is meted out. The aphorism *"justice delayed is justice denied"* proclaimed in Magna Carta in 1215, is sound counsel that should always be borne in mind.

165. The Court must, in the process of hearing a case, vigilantly protect the rights of witnesses reminding them of the right to silence before answering any question which tends to incriminate them. Moreover, the Court must protect the dignity of witnesses against insulting or abusive questions. The oath or affirmation of a witness binds him to answer the questions asked and tell the Court the truth. Telling the truth is, in all ways, the duty of a human being. Lying generally takes one into a false world violating the very substance of being. Lying before the Court is an enemy of justice.

166. If a witness made a previous written statement contrary to his/her testimony, he may be confronted with it and be cross-examined about the contradiction. As a rule, testimony coming in conflict with a previous written statement of a witness is neutralised with sequential consequences on its probative value. Before the Court permits cross-examination of a witness by the party calling him/her, on account of a contradictory previous statement, the witness is declared to be a hostile one.

CHAPTER TWENTY-THREE

FACT-FINDING PROCESS

167. A trial court is responsible for ascertaining the true facts. The fact-finding process involves findings relevant to the credibility of witnesses and evaluation of the evidence adduced before the Court. Procedural rules govern the adduction of evidence under both the adversarial and the inquisitorial systems of justice. The fact-finding process is an important aspect of judgment rendering, its primary object being, to ascertain the facts bearing on the resolution of the issues before the Court. The fact-finding process must be distinguished from the burden of proof. A witness may be believed or disbelieved. It is the domain of the Court to bring judgment to bear on the credibility of a witness. Like every other aspect of the judgment of the Court this process too is subject to due reasoning. Whether the burden of proof prescribed by law is discharged by the party bearing it, is determined by reference to the findings of fact of the Court and the law applicable to the subject.

CHAPTER TWENTY-FOUR

EVALUATION OF REASONABLENESS OF TIME

168. In evaluating the reasonableness of time taken for the determination of judicial proceedings, the following considerations count:

a) the volume of evidence,
b) the complexity of the issues raised for consideration and determination,
c) the acuteness of the legal issues posing for resolution and application.

Unnecessary adjournments no doubt protract the proceedings. If a party unjustifiably delays the proceedings, he/she cannot legitimately complain of the delay in the transaction of the judicial cause. But a party may complain about delays occasioned by the counter party and more so of delays, for which the Court itself is responsible, due either to lack of time or exceedingly leisurely conduct of the proceedings.

The number of judges must at all times be equal to the need for the timely conduct of judicial proceedings. Institutional arrangements must be set up to increase the number of judges as need arises, free of any time consuming process. The Judiciary is in a unique position to assess its manpower needs for the due and expeditious conduct of the proceedings.

Institutional measures must ensure that the judiciary is empowered, as the burden of work warrants, to appoint new judges after due notice to the executive and legislative powers of the state.

169. The need for the timely transaction of judicial proceedings is essential for the appraisal of the parties' rights. Certainty of knowledge about one's rights and liabilities is vital for the planning of one's life and discharge of duties to fellow human beings and the public. Hence, the time within which judicial proceedings are concluded is a consequential factor, not only for the efficacy of the judicial process but equally so for the elicitation of the rights of man.

170. The appellate process must also be conducted expeditiously for similar if not more cogent reasons as the trial of a case. In the inquisitorial system, where the appeal is by way of re-hearing, it must be conducted the soonest possible, bearing in mind, inter alia, that time may weaken the memory of witnesses.

171. In many legal systems, there is a third tier of justice taking the form of a Court of Cassation (Cour de Cassation), or a second level of appeal in common law systems. The jurisdiction of the Court of Cassation is limited to legal issues, not so in the common law systems of justice where an appeal may be raised in respect of any aspect of the issues before the trial court. Recourse to a third tier of justice requires, as a rule, leave from the court; regarded as an exceptional measure. Leave is ordinarily granted only if issues of extraordinary importance arise for ponderation.

172. The need for speed in the conduct of judicial proceedings increases at every new stage of the proceedings, in view of the inevitable prolongation of time for coming to the end of the process.

173. Under the inquisitorial system of justice, the appeal is held by way of rehearing. The court will consider afresh all issues arising in the trial process. Evidently, rehearing is held with hindsight of the nature and complexity of the issues before the Court. Of course, the trial is held anew without any presumptions about the validity of the first instance proceedings or the verdict of the Court.

174. Where the realm of appeal is limited to a review of a first instance judgment, the object is to determine the correctness of the impugned decision. And as the decision is the offspring of the trial, its conduct is also at issue. Immaterial errors, that is, errors that leave the outcome of the case unaffected, leave the verdict of the court intact. To come to such a decision, the court of appeal must be certain that no miscarriage of justice has occurred. Findings of fact of the trial court are binding upon the court of appeal unless manifestly fraught with error. After all, the Court of Appeal does not have the chance to see the witnesses, watch their demeanour and evaluate the coherence of their evidence. Nevertheless, the Court of Appeal may interfere with findings of fact if based on inadmissible evidence or defy reason. A misconception of law or its erroneous application to the resolution of the issues before the court, justifies interference with the decisions of the trial court. No evidence in relation to the subject-matter of the case is receivable on appeal. Uncertainties about the impact of evidence or gaps in it provide no ground for the reception of evidence at that stage of the proceedings. Evidence shedding light on the issues of the case may only be received on appeal if unavailable at the trial to the extent that no reasonable effort by the party seeking its production could bring it to light or secure it.

175. Identification of the relevant principles of the law and their clarification, where necessary, is a major function of the court of appeal. The word

of the higher echelon of the judiciary is treated as an authentic expression of the law on a subject. At an earlier stage, we referred to the principle of binding precedent in common law systems of justice and its present range of application. It must be noticed that the rigidity of the principle of binding precedent in England and common law countries, has been relaxed, following the Practice Statement of the House of Lords of 1966, entitling the final judicial layer of justice to depart from previous decisions of it, if the interests of justice so warrant; in other words, whenever injustice would necessarily follow from the application of the principle.

176. Recently, the English Court of Appeal too, acknowledged a right under specified circumstances, to depart from previous decisions of its own. It laid down that a five-member bench of the Court of Appeal can depart from or overrule a previous decision of the Court of Appeal, emanating from a bench of three appeal judges.

177. If the decision of the trial court is for one or more reasons, legal or factual, considered erroneous, the remedies available to the court of appeal are a reversal of the first instance decision, amendment of it or re-trial.

178. Reversal entails the opposite of the first instance judgment usually signified by the expression "appeal allowed". Amendment entails the modification of the first instance judgment as the decision of the court of appeal warrants. Re-trial denotes what it says, the trial of the case anew. To my mind an order for retrial of a criminal case is not free of problems. It is a fundamental right of man not to be tried twice for an offence in relation to which he was acquitted or found guilty. An order of retrial derives from a finding of the Court of Appeal that the conviction or acquittal is unsafe or unreliable. The rule against double jeopardy (*autre fois acquit, autre fois convict*), is a fundamental human right with a long history marked, to begin, by the Latin maxim *"ne bis in idem"*. If a person cannot be put at risk of conviction twice, re-trial cannot be a remedy available on appeal. The only exception would be if the first trial was, for one or more reasons, a nullity. In that case the person was not at risk of conviction at the trial. A trial held outside the norms of a fair trial or in defiance of them is null and its decision void. Hence, the accused was not at risk of a valid conviction.

179. Even when re-trial is possible because of nullity of the first instance proceedings, re-trial should not be ordered if the time that elapsed makes re-trial of a case within a reasonable time impossible.

CHAPTER TWENTY-FIVE

ELEMENTS OF A REASONED JUDGMENT

180. Rendering a reasoned judgment is an inseverable element of a fair trial. The court is duty bound to reason its decision, every aspect of it, and correspondingly, a litigant has a right to such a judgment. Absence of reasoning in any material respect invalidates the decision inasmuch as it is not the offspring of a fair trial. Reasoning a judgment is not only warranted by the efficacy of the judicial process; it reveals error, of law or fact, if any, committed by the trial Court. A reasoned judgment is a species of accountability of judicial action. Reason is the common denominator by reference to which a position is evaluated. It is what humanity shares in the transaction of its affairs and what can provide validation of a proposition or finding.

181. Reasons must be provided for the conclusions of the court on every material issue before it. Fact-finding must be reasoned not only by reference to belief or disbelief of the testimony of a witness, but by its objective soundness too. Personal impressions gained from the demeanour of a witness is a relevant consideration but not the only one. The evidence of a witness must be assessed in the context of the totality of the evidence and ultimately evaluated by its logicality within the framework of the transaction of human affairs and any individual tendencies or disposition of a witness.

182. Identification of the law applicable is not a complicated affair for a judge. More difficult is the interpretation of the law, the canons of construction of statutes. Not infrequently the wording of a statute is unclear. How do we go about identifying its meaning? As earlier noted, rules have been articulated about the interpretation of statutes such as the grammatical rule, giving to the words used, their ordinary meaning, the purposive or teleological rule, giving to the ends of a statute dominant importance in the interpretation of its provisions. The history of the enactment is another aid to the interpretation of a statute, involving identification of the background to the enactment of the statute, including the travaux preparatoires in the case of treaties, conventions and international agreements. The teleological approach entails reading a provision of the

law within the framework of the purpose of the statute and perceived object of individual provisions of it. The objects of the law are often but not invariably declared in the preamble of a statute. The preamble is not in itself a part of the statute, but a declaration of the ends that the law is intended to serve or remedy.

183. The findings of fact at which the trial court arrives, must be evaluated in the first place, by reference to the party that bears the burden of proof with a view to determining whether he/she has discharged it, the claimant in a civil and the prosecutor in a criminal case. In administrative proceedings the task of the Court is to ascertain, with the participation of the parties, whether the authority against which a recourse is directed has acted within the premises of the law and in accordance with the principles of sound administration. An inquiry is held into the propriety of the contested decision.

CHAPTER TWENTY-SIX

STANDARD OF PROOF IN CRIMINAL CASES

184. Proof beyond any reasonable doubt or beyond any doubt, is the standard of proof in criminal cases. Proof of the guilt of the accused beyond reasonable doubt is acknowledged as a fundamental right of the defendant and, correspondingly, the inextricable duty of the Court to give effect to it. Even where the onus to introduce evidence is cast on the accused, the burden is of an evidential character, discharged by adducing evidence on the subject. The imposition of such an onus on the accused does not shift the general burden of proof. The standard of proof remains unaltered, proof beyond reasonable doubt. The general burden of proof remains throughout on the prosecution. Any doubt about the guilt of the accused, entitles the defendant to acquittal.

185. The presumption of innocence is another fundamental right of the accused, which in itself absolves the defendant of any burden to establish his/her innocence. It is generally accepted that the presumption of innocence requires an adversarial hearing given that the accuser must prove the opposite of what the presumption imports, namely, that the accused is innocent. It is for the accuser to prove the guilt of the accused, not for the Court to inquire into the matter. It is the right of the accused to know in advance the charges laid against him/her and the evidence supporting them. The presumption of innocence pervades the entire criminal trial process.

186. The principle of equality of arms between the prosecution and the defence is deeply rooted. In practice, the means available to the parties to put forward their case are not the same. The prosecution of crime is generally a public affair, the means that the prosecuting authorities have at their disposal are, as a rule, much greater than those available to the accused. Fairness demands that the state should establish an agency for the provision of facilities to the defence to probe into matters relevant to the defence of the accused.

187. The two sides must, in relation to any issue arising in the course of the trial, be given an equal opportunity to present their case before the court. When the case for both parties is closed they must be given a chance

to make final addresses. In criminal cases, as a rule, the defence has the last word, a corollary of the presumption of innocence.

188. Crime and its punishment is a public affair. Crime brings disorder, violates the rights of others and merits the attention of society. The victim, compared to other members of the community, is the person hurt the most. The victim has, and should have the right to raise a private prosecution if the state does not mount one. The rules of procedure and evidence, with respect to a private prosecution are the same as those applicable to a public prosecution. The tenor of the presumption of innocence is, to the same effect as in a public prosecution, so is the burden of proof. Private prosecutions are rare nowadays. Yet, it is a right that should be upheld, as a right that individuates to the victim that justice be done.

189. It must be noticed, that unlike the prosecution, the defence is under no obligation to disclose its case before the trial or in the process of it. Exceptionally, provision is made for the disclosure of defences the facts of which are peculiarly within the knowledge of the accused, such as the defence of alibi or lack of mental capacity to appreciate the consequences of one's acts.

CHAPTER TWENTY-SEVEN

JOINDER OF OFFENCES—JOINDER OF OFFENDERS

190. Offences committed by the same offender within the context of the same criminal transaction are, as a rule, joined in the same indictment. Offences of a similar nature, committed on earlier or subsequent occasions to the central issues of the prosecution, may likewise be joined in the same charge-sheet. The principle is that offences, having a chronological or character nexus between each other can be made the subject of the same prosecution. The number of offences joined in the same indictment must not be unduly long, a fact that inevitably makes preparation for the defence especially onerous. The accused must be assured the right to object, wholly or in part, to the joinder of offences, by reference to the norms of a fair trial and in particular, the possibility of being prejudicially affected by the multiplicity of charges. Discretion must lie with the Court to order disjoinder, if the interests of justice so require.

191. Joinder of offenders in the same indictment is also open to the prosecution. Disjoinder may be ordered on any ground associated with the fairness and efficacy of the judicial process. Difficulties may arise in the advancement of the defence of one or more accused. Another obvious complication is the deciphering of the evidence implicating each one of the co-accused. A relevant consideration in approaching a motion for disjoinder is the likelihood of incriminating evidence steaming from anyone of the co-accused against a fellow accused. A co-accused is under no obligation to inform his fellow accused of any intention to incriminate himself/herself in his/her sworn or unsworn testimony from the dock or through the production of evidence. On the other hand, joinder does save time and may facilitate the presentation of a comprehensive picture of criminal action enabling the Court to appreciate the evidence in its proper perspective. In the case of joinder of offenders, the Court has a difficult task, given that a joint trial must in no way prejudice the rights of any one of the accused. In some legal systems, incriminating evidence by a co-accused is admissible against a fellow accused, subject to the right of the latter to cross-examine the co-accused before the prosecution does so. I entertain great doubts whether this is compatible with the principles of a fair trial and the rights of the accused in this connection. Evidence given

by a co-accused, incriminating his fellow accused, forms no part of the prosecution that the latter has to face, nor is he given notice of such evidence for the preparation of his/her defence. Consequently, reception of such evidence should not count against the incriminated fellow accused. This is an essential safeguard of the right of the accused to a fair trial. The case that each one has to answer is the case put forward by the prosecution. The rules of evidence are not relaxed by the fact that the prosecution is directed against two or more persons. As in the case of joinder of offences, likewise in the case of joinder of offenders, the court must have the right to order separate trials if the interests of justice so demand.

CHAPTER TWENTY-EIGHT

REASONING OF JUDGMENT IN TRIALS BEFORE JUDGE AND JURY

192. Where the judicial bench is mixed, consisting of judges and laymen, the judgment of the court reflects the findings of the bench as a whole and the verdict is reasoned in the way mandated by a fair trial. Questions arise as to the reasoning of the judgment in trials held before judge and jury, as the two distinct components of the trial, which is the case under the English and other common law systems of justice. The judge directs the jury as to the law and sums up the evidence drawing attention to the strength and shortcomings of different parts of it, leaving it to the jury to evaluate the evidence and decide whether the case against the accused has been proven or not. The jury may, before coming to its conclusions, seek clarification of aspects of the summing up or legal assistance with regard to the crucial issues posing for determination. Ultimately, the jury is responsible to return a verdict of guilty or not guilty. Reasons for its decision are not given. Its validity is co-related to the adequacy of the summing up of the judge. The net result is that the jury is the fact-finder, without providing reasons for its findings and, sequentially, its verdict. The inevitable inference is that the judgment of the court is not reasoned. The gap would be filled if the jury gave reasons for its decisions, the soundness of which can be tested on appeal. Trial before judge and jury in civil cases is nowadays a rare phenomenon, in England confined mostly to libel actions. The same reservations are expressed about the compatibility of the verdict of the jury with the norms of a fair trial.

CHAPTER TWENTY-NINE

SENTENCE REASONING

193. Judgment on sentence must likewise be reasoned by reference to factors bearing on the punishment of the convicted person, primarily the gravity of the offence and the person of the accused. The sentence as often said *"must fit the offence and the offender"*. In the latter case, good character counts as a mitigating factor.

CHAPTER THIRTY

BURDEN OF PROOF IN CIVIL CASES

194. As in criminal, so in civil cases, it is for the claimant (plaintiff), the contender, to establish the claim raised. The burden of proof is lighter compared to that applicable to criminal cases, dependent on possibilities, as opposed to certainty in criminal cases. In civil cases too, the findings of fact pave the way for the resolution of the issues before the Court. Preponderance of probabilities is the standard of proof in civil cases. Unlike criminal cases, parties to civil proceedings are under a duty to communicate in advance to each other their position in relation to the subject-matter of the proceedings. The principle of equality of arms is applicable as in criminal cases. The discernment of probabilities is a matter of logic, revealing what is more probable than not. Probability must be distinguished from possibility. As the probability rises, so does the degree of certainty about an occurrence. Comparing the two standards of proof applicable in criminal and civil cases, the outcome is that in the former, the court must be unqualifiedly certain whereas in the latter, relatively so.

CHAPTER THIRTY-ONE

PUNISHMENT OF CRIME

195. Punishment of crime is the exclusive province of the judiciary under every system of justice. According to theocratic belief, punishment of a sin is a Godly affair, save that the sanctions imposed are suffered in the hereafter. The righteous on the other hand, are rewarded by a blessed afterlife. In the living world, punishment of crime is the province of the judiciary. The form and nature of punishment is prescribed by law. As a rule, the law prescribes the maximum punishment that may be imposed leaving the determination of sentence, in any one case, to the Judge.

196. Traditionally, punishment has been viewed as a retribution for the crime committed, giving back to the offender his/her due deserts. It also serves, as often asserted, a second objective, namely, deterrence of the particular offender and potential offenders from engaging in criminal action. As history reveals, the only cases where sentence could be pre-ordained by law, were capital offences, where the death penalty was sanctioned as the sole punishment. Nowadays, it is acknowledged that the right of man not to be subjected to torture, inhuman or degrading treatment, safeguarded as a fundamental human right, rules out the death penalty as a legitimate form of punishment. This position is also consistent with the proposition that punishment is meant to ameliorate not to destroy the person.

197. Deportation, as earlier noted, has been another species of punishment for crime, often imposed by courts in England, in the past, a process incidentally helping in the colonisation by English people of newly found lands. This is again an extinct form of punishment unless one considers the deportation of illegal immigrants a punishment of a similar kind.

198. Reform must be the principal object of punishment with a view to reclaiming a fellow human being as a useful member of society. Education and teaching skills that will provide the offender with the means to earn a living are evident tools of a reformative process. The use of punishment as a means of reform can also find justification in the shortcomings of society, especially failure to provide proper education and neglect of those in need.

199. Over the years, other means of punishment have been evolved that place the accent on reform. A hospital order for drug offenders, aimed to cure their addiction, is another means of humane treatment. Greater emphasis on reform is laid in the case of minor offenders. Sending a child to a reform school is one such method, while placing the minor under supervision of the welfare authorities is the most usual one.

200. Probation is also a reformative measure available in the case of both children and adults, especially young offenders. The convicted person is placed under the supervision of the welfare authorities regulating at the same time, the movements of the probationer in an effort to aid the offender discipline in his/her ways. Giving a recognisance to keep the law is another form of lenient treatment binding over the offender to abide by the law for a specified period of time. In the event of breach of the undertaking given, the recognisance will be forfeited while the person will be prosecuted for the offence causing the breach.

201. A social order is yet another method of treatment of offenders requiring them to do, for a period of time, community work as a means of redressing the wrong done. A suspended sentence of imprisonment for crimes of lesser gravity is a relatively new mode of punishment allied to imprisonment. To impose this sentence the court must in the first place determine that imprisonment is the appropriate punishment. A suspended sentence of imprisonment is not an alternative to a fine or any other form of punishment. Suspension aims to give the offender a chance not to forfeit his/her liberty. If during the period of suspension the culprit commits another offence, the sentence of imprisonment can be activated and in addition thereto, punishment may be imposed for the new offence.

202. It is generally acknowledged that sentence must fit both the offence and the offender. The person of the accused, his/her criminal record, if any, expressions and most significantly deeds evincing remorse, such as payment of compensation or readiness to pay for the injury occasioned, loss or damage sustained by the victim, constitute mitigating factors. Also, deeds for the public good are relevant in the determination of sentence. In conventional terms, acts elicited above, count in mitigation of sentence.

203. Retribution, that is requital for the crime committed, is a means of punishment for its own sake, giving back to the offender what is due to him/her. However, it cannot be welcome as the principal reason for

punishment. Confining a person to prison simpliciter, may have negative repercussions, unless accompanied by processes designed to uplift and elevate the knowledge and ethos of the offender. Education of the prisoner, especially education about the ethics of justice is a most salutary process in addressing criminal tendencies of the detainee. Teaching a prisoner a skill is another way of enabling the detainee to follow new ways of life after release. Therapy of persons suffering from mental or bodily afflictions may well restore a prisoner as an active member of society. Detention merely for the sake of confinement may have the opposite effect to reform. Companionship with fellow criminals may well intensify the propensity to crime. Lack of communication with the outside world again, may dangerously isolate or estrange the person. Periodic exit from prison helps moderate the effects of alienating the prisoner from the social corpus.

204. I am in no position to determine the extent to which the prospect of punishment serves as a deterrent. Punishment entails consequences for the offender involving, as a rule, loss of liberty and/or financial penalties that undoubtedly constitute a prohibitive factor. On the other hand, this fear is conducive to prospective offenders innovating new criminal methods to avoid capture. The extent to which fear of punishment may serve as a deterrent is a very complex question. Arguments may be advanced either way.

205. The fundamental right of equality of human beings, entails equality of treatment of persons in the same or similar position. This is the universal duty of every authority of the State, preeminently the judiciary. Here, as elsewhere, equality signifies homogeneity of subjects and objects of the law, not arithmetical equality. Hence, elements distinguishing the position of the aforesaid category of offenders may justify differentiation of the punishment of those convicted. Any favour shown to any one of them by the prosecutorial or any other authority of the state does constitute a factor bearing on the treatment of the co-accused by the judiciary.

CHAPTER THIRTY-TWO

PROCEDURAL RULES

206. Procedural rules must be attuned to the norms of a fair trial, taking into account the particularities of each field of the judicial process. The period for counting reasonable time in judicial proceedings commences with the start of police investigations into the case or the arrest of the accused. In civil proceedings, time begins to count from the date of initiation of the proceedings. A question may arise, in the latter case, as to the adequacy of the rule for the following reasons: Should it not also be correlated to the time that the cause of action accrued to the knowledge of the plaintiff? In criminal cases too, noticeable delay to report a crime should also count unless lapse of time thereto is duly explained. Take a hypothetical case, a cause of action accrues to the knowledge of the claimant on day one. An action is raised five years later, within the period of prescription, if there is any, without any explanation being offered for the lapse of time, such as meeting a request of the prospective defendant to give him time for making redress. To my mind, the date of accrual of the cause of action to the knowledge of the vestee of the right should be treated as a relevant consideration in determining the reasonableness of time for the ascertainment of the rights and duties of the parties to litigation. After all, knowledge of one's rights and awareness of liabilities is essential for peace of mind and planning one's affairs.

207. In civil proceedings, knowledge of the position of either side in advance to the hearing of the case, is postulated as a vital step of the process. Hence in civil proceedings, the response of the defendant is highly relevant to the identification of the issues posing for resolution.

208. In criminal proceedings, not only the charge(s) must be communicated to the accused in advance, but the evidence to be adduced in support of the case must also be disclosed. No corresponding duty is cast on the defendant to communicate his defence to the prosecutorial side. As earlier indicated, there are exceptions to this rule, in relation to a defence the facts of which are within the peculiar knowledge of the accused.

CHAPTER THIRTY-THREE

EPILOGUE

209. Justice is an all-embracive concept and discipline encompassing every aspect of life. The rules of justice aim to harmonize the unitary but often conflicting nature of man as a natural and social entity with emphasis on the development of the potential of the individual. There is cross-influence between the constituent elements of a human being. Man is subject to natural and social forces. The two interact. Justice aims to bring a balance between the zoic (animalistic) and political side of man. The deeply rooted instinct of self-preservation inclines man to look after his/her being and those near and dear to the individual. Untrammeled devotion to this tendency may be destructive and lead to egocentricity. Justice aims to balance this inclination by the cultivation of another inborn tendency of man, fellowship. Man is a product of nature and must live in harmony with the environment. Man is a political being. Individuality and communality must coexist in harmony. Room must be provided for the advancement of the faculties of man that enable the individual to attain his/her potential.

210. Decisions and actions of the collectivity on the other hand must be balanced by the recognition of the autonomy of each part of it, the individual. The collectivity should never submerge or suppress its component parts. It must act as a collective, not as an independent, force. It must always leave space for the individual to propound his/her point of view, and room for its expression. The individuality of man must be sustained and communality must reflect that.

211. Human rights are designed to harmonise the rights of man with those of the collectivity, making up the state. The duties inherent in man and those of the corporate human estate are designed to bring about an equilibrium between rights and duties. Individualism is moderated by a sense of collegiality. Knowledge revealing the interdependence of individuals enhances the understanding of the benefits of cooperative action that underline the common fate of humanity. Knowledge about nature and implications of human action on the environment is highly beneficial, paving the way for the use of land in harmony with nature. After all, the right to life confers a say to man on the shaping of the environment enveloping human existence.

212. Human rights assure the individual of what befits human nature. This is reflected in their universality and the entitlement of every human being to their enjoyment. They embrace every facet of human life in the public and private domain. Human rights import a corresponding duty to heed the parallel rights of every other person. They also cast a duty on state authorities to take account of and give effect to them in every sphere of life. Respect for the indistinguishable rights of fellow human beings is a fundamental precept of human rights. Respect for the identical human rights of fellow human beings is a duty imported by the very nature of human rights. It is inexorably unjust to enjoy rights denied to fellow human beings. Rights entail obligations of equal significance to the rights conferred upon the individual. Denial or disregard of these obligations is antinomous to the very concept of rights.

213. Ultimately, justice is tied to the good of humanity, individually and collectively.

214. Law, as already indicated, was perceived as the means of giving practical effect to justice; its agent. Democracy as a system of governance sprung, as explained, from the basic norms of justice. History informs that, over the centuries, law has often been used by rulers as a means of suppressing people in the interest of their sustenance in power and the perpetuation of their hegemony. Megalomania is the principal characteristic of such rulers, not infrequently accompanied by commitment to concepts of perceived infallibility.

215. It must be noticed that what activated the clamour for change of misanthropic regimes, was invariably the absence of justice. In due course, the acknowledgment of human rights with what it entails, filled shortfalls in political systems. Acknowledgment is one thing, incorporation into the legal system of a country or region, another. Much is worldwide missing in this area.

216. The subject of human rights is the individual without distinction wherever in the world he/she is to be found or resides. One may conclude that laws falling short of the dictates of justice, encountered in brutal regimes, are bound to be amended or banished depending on the magnitude of the deviation.

217. History tells that regimes mostly of a totalitarian nature that functioned outside the realm of justice have brought human misery and distraction on a gigantic scale. Every form of rule outside the norms of justice is and has been detrimental to humanity.

218. Just rule is what sustains man, lays the ground for the advancement of the individual and enhancement of the collectivity. Rules of justice are founded on what is good for man at present and foreseeably in the future. They are fashioned to the ends of life diachronically. Law is the means of incorporating the commands of justice into social order accompanied by a variety of sanctions for breaches of its provisions. Sanctions too must conform to the dictates of justice congenial to human nature and never destructive.

219. Obedience to the law is an edict of justice contributing thereby to the establishment of the rule of law, acknowledging law and not any person or group of persons as the supreme authority in a state. The backbone of the rule of law is the judiciary. Judicial mechanisms must be present to ensure conformity of legislation to the basic norms of justice with power vested in the judiciary to declare offensive legislation unenforceable as a whole, or offensive provisions of it.

220. Philanthropy signifying, in the original Greek sense of the word, love of humanity is one of the cornerstones of justice.

221. A question often asked is this;. is human nature prone to act justly? History provides conflicting evidence revealing tendencies of man in either direction. Can the negative tendencies of man be moderated- is there a way? The answer to the question is positive. Man's spiritual capacities have, as one may gather, no limit. By cultivating this capacity through the acquisition of knowledge, steered by commitment to truth, man can understand, grasp and appreciate that justice is the superior norm of life. Hence, man is gifted with the ability to appreciate universal norms beneficial to the individual and society. What can be supported is that when man pursues knowledge without hinderance, free from dogmatic preconceptions, he/she is up to act justly.

222. As the law was meant to be the agent of justice, so the judiciary was conceived as the guardian of justice. Dispensing justice is a mission of a most delicate character. Suffering injustice is perhaps the most traumatic experience man can undergo. Affirmation of justice and remedying injustice is the principal function of the judiciary. Acknowledgment of rights when disputed is another part of its mission. Disowning laws breaching the corpus of justice, safeguarded by a constitution or a basic law, emphasises its mission as the guardian of justice.

223. The independence and impartiality of the judiciary as well as its separateness and distance from the other powers of the state and every

source of power are all important, fundamental to the fulfillment of its mission. A judiciary living up to its mission is the fountainhead of society generating confidence in that life becomes meaningful, the rights of man are dully protected, bringing about happiness and opening the gates to the creativity of man.

224. In sum, justice is what ensures the harmonious and beneficial coexistence of mankind and lays the ground for life in harmony with nature.

225. At any one time, justice lays the ground for harmonious coexistence of human beings in society, with the ever coming tomorrow in sight. Justice generates respect for human beings, cultivates fellowship in society and demands lasting respect for nature that sustains humanity.

226. Living according to the tenets of justice brings happiness and enables man to realise his/her infinite potential. In sum, justice is the raison d' être of life, the premise of cosmic order.

ANNEX

THE UNIVERSAL DECLARATION OF HUMAN RIGHTS

Preamble

Whereas recognition of the inherent dignity and of the equal and inalienable rights of all members of the human family is the foundation of freedom, justice and peace in the world,

Whereas disregard and contempt for human rights have resulted in barbarous acts which have outraged the conscience of mankind, and the advent of a world in which human beings shall enjoy freedom of speech and belief and freedom from fear and want has been proclaimed as the highest aspiration of the common people,

Whereas it is essential, if man is not to be compelled to have recourse, as a last resort, to rebellion against tyranny and oppression, that human rights should be protected by the rule of law,

Whereas it is essential to promote the development of friendly relations between nations,

Whereas the peoples of the United Nations have in the Charter reaffirmed their faith in fundamental human rights, in the dignity and worth of the human person and in the equal rights of men and women and have determined to promote social progress and better standards of life in larger freedom,

Whereas Member States have pledged themselves to achieve, in co-operation with the United Nations, the promotion of universal respect for and observance of human rights and fundamental freedoms,

Whereas a common understanding of these rights and freedoms is of the greatest importance for the full realization of this pledge,

Now, Therefore THE GENERAL ASSEMBLY proclaims THIS UNIVERSAL DECLARATION OF HUMAN RIGHTS as a common standard of achievement for all peoples and all nations, to the end that every individual and every organ of society, keeping this Declaration constantly in mind, shall strive by teaching and education to promote respect for these rights and freedoms and by progressive measures, national and international, to secure their universal and effective recognition and observance, both among the peoples of Member States themselves and among the peoples of territories under their jurisdiction.

Article 1

All human beings are born free and equal in dignity and rights. They are endowed with reason and conscience and should act towards one another in a spirit of brotherhood.

Article 2

Everyone is entitled to all the rights and freedoms set forth in this Declaration, without distinction of any kind, such as race, colour, sex, language, religion, political or other opinion, national or social origin, property, birth or other status. Furthermore, no distinction shall be made on the basis of the political, jurisdictional or international status of the country or territory to which a person belongs, whether it be independent, trust, non-self-governing or under any other limitation of sovereignty.

Article 3

Everyone has the right to life, liberty and security of person.

Article 4

No one shall be held in slavery or servitude; slavery and the slave trade shall be prohibited in all their forms.

Article 5

No one shall be subjected to torture or to cruel, inhuman or degrading treatment or punishment.

Article 6

Everyone has the right to recognition everywhere as a person before the law.

Article 7

All are equal before the law and are entitled without any discrimination to equal protection of the law. All are entitled to equal protection against any discrimination in violation of this Declaration and against any incitement to such discrimination.

Article 8

Everyone has the right to an effective remedy by the competent national tribunals for acts violating the fundamental rights granted him by the constitution or by law.

Article 9

No one shall be subjected to arbitrary arrest, detention or exile.

Article 10

Everyone is entitled in full equality to a fair and public hearing by an independent and impartial tribunal, in the determination of his rights and obligations and of any criminal charge against him.

Article 11

(1) Everyone charged with a penal offence has the right to be presumed innocent until proved guilty according to law in a public trial at which he has had all the guarantees necessary for his defence.
(2) No one shall be held guilty of any penal offence on account of any act or omission which did not constitute a penal offence, under national or international law, at the time when it was committed. Nor shall a heavier penalty be imposed than the one that was applicable at the time the penal offence was committed.

Article 12

No one shall be subjected to arbitrary interference with his privacy, family, home or correspondence, nor to attacks upon his honour and reputation. Everyone has the right to the protection of the law against such interference or attacks.

Article 13

(1) Everyone has the right to freedom of movement and residence within the borders of each state.
(2) Everyone has the right to leave any country, including his own, and to return to his country.

Article 14

(1) Everyone has the right to seek and to enjoy in other countries asylum from persecution.
(2) This right may not be invoked in the case of prosecutions genuinely arising from non-political crimes or from acts contrary to the purposes and principles of the United Nations.

Article 15

(1) Everyone has the right to a nationality.
(2) No one shall be arbitrarily deprived of his nationality nor denied the right to change his nationality.

Article 16

(1) Men and women of full age, without any limitation due to race, nationality or religion, have the right to marry and to found a family. They are entitled to equal rights as to marriage, during marriage and at its dissolution.
(2) Marriage shall be entered into only with the free and full consent of the intending spouses.
(3) The family is the natural and fundamental group unit of society and is entitled to protection by society and the State.

Article 17

(1) Everyone has the right to own property alone as well as in association with others.
(2) No one shall be arbitrarily deprived of his property.

Article 18

Everyone has the right to freedom of thought, conscience and religion; this right includes freedom to change his religion or belief, and freedom, either alone or in community with others and in public or private, to manifest his religion or belief in teaching, practice, worship and observance.

Article 19

Everyone has the right to freedom of opinion and expression; this right includes freedom to hold opinions without interference and to seek, receive and impart information and ideas through any media and regardless of frontiers.

Article 20

(1) Everyone has the right to freedom of peaceful assembly and association.
(2) No one may be compelled to belong to an association.

Article 21

(1) Everyone has the right to take part in the government of his country, directly or through freely chosen representatives.
(2) Everyone has the right of equal access to public service in his country.
(3) The will of the people shall be the basis of the authority of government; this will shall be expressed in periodic and genuine elections which shall be by universal and equal suffrage and shall be held by secret vote or by equivalent free voting procedures.

Article 22

Everyone, as a member of society, has the right to social security and is entitled to realization, through national effort and international co-operation and in accordance with the organization and resources of each State, of the economic, social and cultural rights indispensable for his dignity and the free development of his personality.

Article 23

(1) Everyone has the right to work, to free choice of employment, to just and favourable conditions of work and to protection against unemployment.
(2) Everyone, without any discrimination, has the right to equal pay for equal work.
(3) Everyone who works has the right to just and favourable remuneration ensuring for himself and his family an existence worthy of human dignity, and supplemented, if necessary, by other means of social protection.
(4) Everyone has the right to form and to join trade unions for the protection of his interests.

Article 24

Everyone has the right to rest and leisure, including reasonable limitation of working hours and periodic holidays with pay.

Article 25

(1) Everyone has the right to a standard of living adequate for the health and well-being of himself and of his family, including food, clothing, housing and medical

care and necessary social services, and the right to security in the event of unemployment, sickness, disability, widowhood, old age or other lack of livelihood in circumstances beyond his control.
(2) Motherhood and childhood are entitled to special care and assistance. All children, whether born in or out of wedlock, shall enjoy the same social protection.

Article 26

(1) Everyone has the right to education. Education shall be free, at least in the elementary and fundamental stages. Elementary education shall be compulsory. Technical and professional education shall be made generally available and higher education shall be equally accessible to all on the basis of merit.
(2) Education shall be directed to the full development of the human personality and to the strengthening of respect for human rights and fundamental freedoms. It shall promote understanding, tolerance and friendship among all nations, racial or religious groups, and shall further the activities of the United Nations for the maintenance of peace.
(3) Parents have a prior right to choose the kind of education that shall be given to their children.

Article 27

(1) Everyone has the right freely to participate in the cultural life of the community, to enjoy the arts and to share in scientific advancement and its benefits.
(2) Everyone has the right to the protection of the moral and material interests resulting from any scientific, literary or artistic production of which he is the author.

Article 28

Everyone is entitled to a social and international order in which the rights and freedoms set forth in this Declaration can be fully realized.

Article 29

(1) Everyone has duties to the community in which alone the free and full development of his personality is possible.
(2) In the exercise of his rights and freedoms, everyone shall be subject only to such limitations as are determined by law solely for the purpose of securing due recognition and respect for the rights and freedoms of others and of meeting the

just requirements of morality, public order and the general welfare in a democratic society.
(3) These rights and freedoms may in no case be exercised contrary to the purposes and principles of the United Nations.

ARTICLE 30

Nothing in this Declaration may be interpreted as implying for any State, group or person any right to engage in any activity or to perform any act aimed at the destruction of any of the rights and freedoms set forth herein.

INDEX

www.ingramcontent.com/pod-product-compliance
Lightning Source LLC
Chambersburg PA
CBHW031328230926
51848CB00001B/135
9789004232389